HOW TO BUILD A HUMAN

In Seven Evolutionary Steps

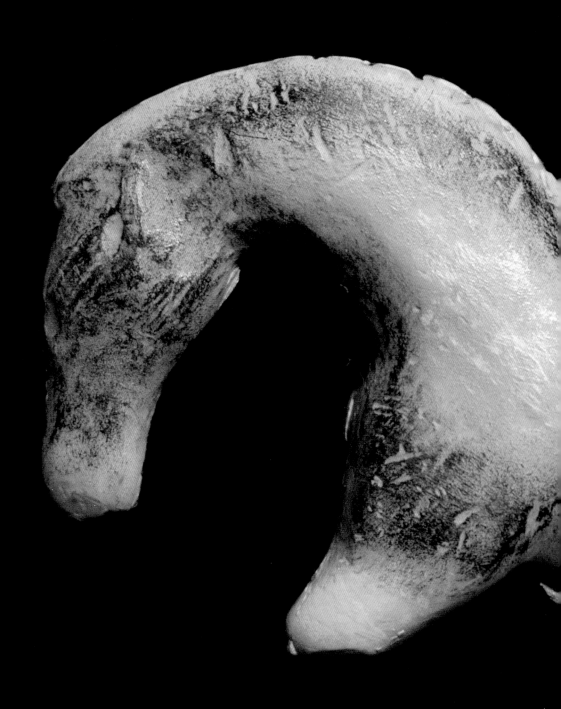

*The Vogelherd Horse from Germany (western Europe),
34,000 to 30,000 years old, carved from mammoth ivory.*

HOW TO BUILD A HUMAN

In Seven Evolutionary Steps

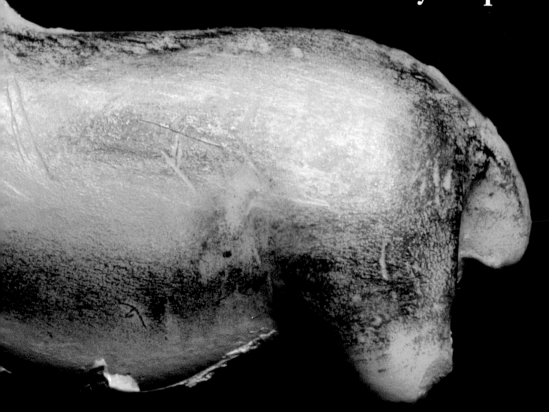

Pamela S. Turner • *Art by* John Gurche

ini Charlesbridge

For Shepherd—P. S. T.

Dedicated to my daughter Blythe, who has surpassed me in all things artistic—J. G.

Published by Charlesbridge
9 Galen Street
Watertown, MA 02472
(617) 926-0329
www.charlesbridge.com

Library of Congress Cataloging-in-Publication Data
Names: Turner, Pamela S., author. | Gurche, John, illustrator.
Title: How to build a human: in seven evolutionary steps / Pamela S. Turner;
    illustrated by John Anthony Gurche.
Description: Watertown, MA: Charlesbridge, 2022. | Includes bibliographical references.
    | Audience: Ages 10+ | Summary: "A celebrated science writer draws upon the most
    recent discoveries in paleoanthropology and evolutionary biology to present the seven
    most important steps leading to *Homo sapiens*."—Provided by publisher.
Identifiers: LCCN 2020052041 (print) | LCCN 2020052042 (ebook) |
    ISBN 9781623542504 (hardcover) | ISBN 9781632897732 (ebook)
Subjects: LCSH: Human evolution—Juvenile literature. | *Homo erectus*—Juvenile
    literature.
Classification: LCC GN281 .T87 2022 (print) | LCC GN281 (ebook) |
    DDC 599.93/8—dc23
LC record available at https://lccn.loc.gov/2020052041
LC ebook record available at https://lccn.loc.gov/2020052042

Printed in China
(hc) 10 9 8 7 6 5 4 3 2

Display type set in Le Havre Hand by Jeremy Dooley
Text type set in Adobe Caslon Pro by Adobe Systems Incorporated
Printed by 1010 Printing International Limited in Huizhou, Guangdong, China
Production supervision by Jennifer Most Delaney
Designed by Diane M. Earley

CONTENTS

FOREWORD

DR. HABIBA CHIRCHIR, PALEOANTHROPOLOGIST IN THE DEPARTMENT OF BIOLOGICAL SCIENCES AT MARSHALL UNIVERSITY AND RESEARCH ASSOCIATE IN HUMAN ORIGINS PROGRAM TEAM, SMITHSONIAN INSTITUTION

Dr. Habiba Chirchir.

I read Pamela Turner's *How to Build a Human* from the perspective of a researcher, teacher, and life-long student of human evolution. From this vantage, I appreciated how Pam portrays key human evolutionary concepts in an easily accessible style. She describes the discoveries of paleo-anthropologists across the world, who locate and study a wide range of evidence in their journey to understand human prehistory. She tells the human story in a personable fashion, accompanying the evidence with vivid descriptions that allow readers to envision ourselves in the story of our ancestors' challenges, resilience, and creativity. She also offers a cultural context for human evolution, exploring the complex symbolic behavior of our ancestors, who, like us, made tools, jewelry, and art.

Evolutionary theory is a scientifically and globally accepted theory supported by years of rigorous research and data accumulation. Human evolution falls within the purview of this broader theory. The evidence supporting human evolutionary theory has been amassed through international collaboration among researchers around the world, all applying rigorous and repeated testing of hypotheses, as this book points out. Paleoanthropologists, like any other scientists, may challenge and disagree with specific hypotheses, but there is consensus among them that the first modern humans evolved in the African continent. Some migrated on to populate Eurasia, Australia, and the Americas, while others remained in the African continent. Pam's book illustrates these ideas unequivocally.

How to Build a Human also speaks to our current public dialogue surrounding the issue of human variation, or so-called race. If all humans are of one species, then why do we observe so much variation within that species? Pam answers this question by presenting the most up-to-date scientific evidence of the geographical and environmental factors that played a role in shaping observed human variation. She does not shy away from chronicling how that variation has been co-opted in ways that have been harmful to those considered "other." Her book helps the reader understand how paleoanthropologists from different cultures and back-grounds continue to work together to reconstruct an inclusive story of humanity and to dismantle the notions of "otherness" that were used to justify colonialism and slavery in the past.

I also read the book as a Kenyan who was reared in the Great Rift Valley, where much of the fossil evidence presented in the book was recovered. The text's vivid descriptions remind me of my home as well as my time in the field working as an academic uncovering fossil remains of our ancestors. As I reminisce about the ground of my youth and the land of our forebears, I also gain a broader and longer perspective of my infini-tesimally small place in the long history of humanity. This allows me to consider myself both as a Kenyan and East African living in the United States and as part of a much larger global society that was and remains highly interconnected. I hope that reading this book will remind us all that we are cosmopolitan citizens of the world.

INTRODUCTION

Imagine that 3 million years ago, an intelligent life-form visits our planet, seeking the brainiest species on Earth for their intergalactic zoo. They would choose a human ancestor, right?

Wrong. Those alien explorers would zoom off with a dolphin.

If those fictional extraterrestrials returned today, they might be stunned to discover that an animal once second-class in the smarts department had evolved into a species that builds cities, makes war, and transmits thoughts from one brain to another brain using little black marks on paper.

Maybe the returning aliens would say: "What a difference a few million years makes!"[1]

How to Build a Human is the story of how we came to be. It's the tale of our extended family, our direct ancestors as well as our cousins. Our ancestors and cousins weren't exactly like us. Most of them couldn't speak. Their most important possessions were broken rocks. But like us they enjoyed the warmth of the morning sun on their cheeks, the taste of honey on their tongue, and the reassurance of a friend's hug. Like us they feared poisonous snakes and creatures with big teeth lunging out of the darkness. Like us they had to deal with whatever life threw at them.

We humans—*Homo sapiens*—are just one of the millions of species that have evolved on this planet during the last 3.6 billion years. Each

---

1   Or "Can you *believe* how they trashed the place?"

creature has taken its own winding evolutionary path. The ancestors of dolphins and whales were land animals that entered the sea; ants and bees took social living to extraordinary extremes; and some parasites evolved the ability to hijack other animals' brains.[2]

Yet out of all these evolutionary stories, ours is possibly the weirdest.

---

2   Such as a one-celled creature that makes rats want to cozy up to cats and a parasitic worm that turns snails into "disco zombies." I am not making this stuff up.

An ancient African ape that lived 20 to 17 million years ago. Like modern great apes such as chimpanzees and gorillas, this ancient ape probably had a dark face and dark fur with pinkish-white skin underneath. Skulls of other ancient and modern primates are shown at the top.

HOW WE STARTED

Go to a zoo and watch the chimps, bonobos, gorillas, and orangutans. Eventually you'll see something—perhaps a mother comforting a wailing infant—that makes you think: "Oh, look at that! They're so *human*!"

Well, yes, any human would think so. That's because we're so *ape*.

Life on Earth probably began with self-copying molecules. Some of those self-copying molecules eventually became single-celled blobs, some of which eventually became multi-cellular blobs, some of which eventually became weird gooey sea creatures, some of which eventually became fish. Some of those fish shimmied out of the sea, eventually becoming land-dwelling lizard-like creatures. Some of those lizard-like creatures branched off to become the dinosaurs, while others became the first mammals, little creatures about as glamorous as rats.

After the demise of the dinosaurs 66 million years ago,[1] we mammals were among the leftovers. We had room to spread out. Our part of the mammal family tree became the primates (monkeys, apes, lemurs, lorises, and tarsiers). We primates evolved in a rain-forest environment. Forward-facing eyes gave us good depth perception, so we could snap up flying insects. Color vision allowed us to spy ripe fruit amid the forest greenery. Our nimble hands with nails (rather than claws) let us peel fruit and pick open seedpods. Those same grasping hands, along with our rotating shoulder joints, were useful for catching swaying branches as we scampered through the trees.

---

1   Mammals owe the giant meteor that extinguished the dinosaurs a thank-you card.

Just as our bodies are rooted in our primate past, so are our minds. Primates are social animals: we play, fight, cuddle, and groom each other. We learn from each other, compete with each other, and cooperate with each other. We crave companionship. Isolation from others is a punishment.

What drove this long, slow slog from self-copying molecules to blobs of cells to gooey sea beasties to the first primates to us? What process built humans and every other kind of creature on Earth?

A Short (I Promise) Side Trip into Evolution

Species evolve—that is, change over time—through the process of natural selection. Natural selection acts on biological traits that are passed from one generation to another through genes. Genes, which are made of chains of molecules known as DNA, are a chemical instruction manual for how to build an organism.

Every time two parents have offspring, their genes are copied and reshuffled and a new variation is produced. Unless you have an identical twin, you and your siblings will have different combinations of genes. Maybe you have your mother's nose and your father's eyes, but your sister and brother have a different assortment of family features. It's the same with other species. Every robin in a nest, every wolf pup in a litter, and every baby spider in an egg sac will have slightly different traits than its siblings.

Besides the variations produced when genes are reshuffled, there are also variations caused by small DNA copying errors. These are called mutations. Every single one of us has around thirty to fifty copying errors in our genome (our collection of genes). Most of these mutations make absolutely no difference. But some do. Varying traits—whether produced by mutations or gene reshuffling—are the raw material of evolution.

As each baby robin, wolf pup, and infant spider lives and grows, it is tested by its environment. Is the robin alert enough to avoid the hawk? Is the wolf fast enough to catch a deer? Does the spider produce a web of sufficient stickiness? If the robin, wolf, or spider has helpful genetic traits (quick reflexes, strong muscles, stomach glands that produce webs of the right gluey-ness), then the animal will be more likely to survive and leave behind offspring of its own. Those helpful traits will spread through the robin population, wolf population, or spider population. Traits likely to result in an early death will not be passed on.

If you remember only one thing about evolution, remember this: *the environment tests and the environment selects.*

Imagine a group of gorillas living in the cool, wet, high-altitude forests of east-central Africa. The male has particularly dense hair for

A group of mountain gorillas.

keeping warm. One of the females in his group has thinner hair but an extra-strong immune system for fighting off disease. Of their four offspring, one has thick hair and a so-so immune system, one has thin hair and a so-so immune system, one has thick hair and an extra-strong immune system, and one has thin hair and an extra-strong immune system. You can probably guess which of these four is most likely to survive and pass its helpful traits to the next generation. You can also probably guess which one is most likely to die young. When this selection process happens generation after generation, the result will be a population of gorillas with thick hair and the ability to fend off many diseases.

But not necessarily *all* diseases. Just as gorillas are constantly undergoing natural selection, so are populations of viruses, bacteria, and parasites. The ones best able to overcome the defenses of their host will pass on those traits to their descendants. The life cycles of many disease-causing organisms are often very short, which allows them to evolve new traits very quickly. That's why multiple variants of the COVID-19 virus appeared as the disease spread around the world.

Evolution through natural selection is sometimes called "survival of the fittest." This makes it sound as if being the biggest and brawniest is always better. Not so. In evolution, "fitness" is measured only by the number of surviving offspring. "Fitness" sometimes means being bigger and stronger. But it can also mean being better at digesting a certain type of food or behaving in a certain kind of way. If one elephant is a devoted mother and leaves behind four offspring that also become parents, her genes will have a bigger impact on the next generation than those of an indifferent mother that raises only one calf.

Countless, ever-changing environments have been testing and selecting creatures over the course of billions of years. Some creatures, such as bacteria, don't appear to have changed very much. But don't let looks fool you. Modern bacteria have been evolving for billions of years. As a result they're extremely good at surviving in their mini-environments (like your stomach).

Testing and selecting over long periods of time sent other creatures down different evolutionary paths, and their descendants branched off to follow yet other pathways. Some lines of descent went extinct; others continued to change. The result of the process of evolution is the incredible diversity of life on planet Earth. Including us—*Homo sapiens*.

So here we are on the great tree of life on Earth. We're swinging on the primate branch, clustered alongside our fellow great apes: chimps, bonobos, gorillas, and orangutans. Yet we look and act very different from our hairy cousins. Why?

Our first big step toward becoming human was exactly that: a step.

A male Australopithecus afarensis *(left) and a male* Australopithecus africanus *(right). Both kinds of Australopiths could walk upright yet were still decent tree climbers.*

STEP 1
WE STAND UP

Look around. Out of over 6,000 mammal species, how many regularly walk (rather than hop) on two legs?

Answer: just us. Giraffes with their goofy necks and elephants with their absurd noses have nothing on humans. We are truly strange.

Around 8 million years ago, our remote ancestors were apes living in a vast rain forest stretching across Africa. The continent's crust slowly cracked. As the pieces pulled apart, the land in between sank, creating the East African Rift System, a series of steep-edged rift valleys along the eastern side of the continent. As the landscape shifted, so did rainfall patterns. What had once been a seamless jungle became a patchwork of woodland, scrub, and grassland threaded by rivers and dappled with lakes and marshes.

Sometime around 7 to 6 million years ago, the forest apes split into two groups. To the west, where the rain forest remained, the forest apes went on living much as they had before. Some of those apes eventually evolved into modern chimpanzees and bonobos. (Chimps and bonobos are our closest relatives in the animal kingdom; we are equally closely related to both, genetically speaking.)

In other parts of Africa, however, where the forest disappeared, the apes could not go on living as they had before. We descend from forest apes that lost their forest.

Modern chimpanzees live mostly in forests. Their clutching feet are an adaptation for tree climbing.

Year after year, millennium after millennium, the environment in Africa's rift valleys tested all the creatures that lived there. Traits that helped a creature survive and reproduce spread through the population. Eventually all these changes added up to a new population that was different enough from its ancestors to be considered a new species.

Former forest antelopes evolved into antelope species with teeth and guts adapted to the tough grasses of the plains and woodlands. Predator populations changed, too. Three kinds of saber-toothed cats evolved: one the size of a leopard, one the size of a lion, and one so big that our ancient ancestor—if inclined—could've walked up on its two legs and looked the giant cat in the eye.[1]

It might seem incredible that former forest apes survived in a more open landscape full of large predators. Many species can't adapt, or can't adapt quickly enough, when their environment changes significantly. They go extinct. But our ancestors had four important things going for them.

ADVANTAGE #1: THEY WERE NOT PICKY EATERS

Like modern chimps, our forest-ape ancestor probably ate fruits, nuts, leaves, insects, honey, and occasionally meat. (Chimp populations have

---

1   An inclination unlikely to be passed to the next generation, if you know what I mean.

also been evolving over the past 7 to 6 million years, of course. But because chimps live mainly in rain-forest habitats, scientists believe chimps look and act more like our common forest-ape ancestor than we do.)

The varied landscape in Africa's rift valleys offered lots of different foods: fish swimming in shallow pools, roots buried in the sand, nestling birds, dried seedpods. Once in a while our ancient ancestors discovered a big treasure, like a three-toed horse carcass covered in saber-toothed cat spit that had been marinating in the sun for three days.

Did I mention they were not picky eaters?

ADVANTAGE #2: THEY SOLVED PROBLEMS TO GET THEIR FOOD

Our forest-ape ancestors were "extractive foragers." An extractive forager survives by figuring out how to get food that is nutritious but takes effort to acquire. Our forest-ape ancestors, just like modern chimps, were no doubt adept at peeling fruits, cracking nuts, tearing seedpods, digging out grubs, and smashing open beehives. Extractive foragers also need good memories because many foods are available only in certain places at certain times of the year. *When will the figs be ripe? Where can I find wild cucumbers?* In the varied habitats of the rift valleys, these problem-solving skills were a matter of life and death.

ADVANTAGE #3: THEY STUCK TOGETHER

Modern chimps and bonobos usually move around in groups, and our forest-ape ancestors probably did so as well. Being social was especially helpful in open areas with few trees to climb. A predator that might easily pick off a lone ape would be more cautious about approaching a band of thirty.

ADVANTAGE #4: THEY COULD ALREADY STAND ON TWO LEGS

Evolution works upon whatever is at hand. What was at hand 7 million years ago was a problem-solving, group-living forest ape with a broad idea about what was edible and the ability to move in a variety of ways—including on two legs.

It's unclear how far back our upright stance goes. Several kinds of apes that lived about 12 to 10 million years ago might have clambered through trees while standing upright and hanging on to branches with their arms. Modern chimps and bonobos sometimes move this way in the trees, even though they knuckle-walk on the ground. Was our last common ancestor with chimps and bonobos mostly a knuckle-walker or mostly a branch-walker? Or was it equally adept at both? We just don't know.

Moving around on two legs has multiple benefits. Once our forest-ape ancestors found themselves living in open spaces, their ability to stand allowed them to more easily scan their surroundings for food or predators. An upright ape also looks bigger than one on all fours—and looking bigger might help scare off a predator or a rival ape. And standing keeps an ape cooler because less of its body's surface falls under the direct glare of the sun.

Standing was helpful. Two-legged walking was even better. For one thing, it uses less energy than knuckle-walking. Walking also leaves hands free to carry a baby, fling a stick at a snake, or gather berries and seedpods from overhead branches.

If the environment favors the survival of those individuals best at standing and moving around on two legs, then those individuals will leave

Sahelanthropus tchadensis lived 7 to 6 million years ago and may have been the first ape to regularly move around on two legs.

behind more offspring. Their advantageous traits—slightly thicker leg bones, slightly flatter feet—will spread through the population. Eventually, after many generations, a new species may evolve.

Scientists have found bits of fossilized bones from three different types of apes that lived from 7 to 5.2 million years ago: *Sahelanthropus tchadensis*, *Orrorin tugenensis*, and *Ardipithecus kadabba*. Sahel, Orrorin, and Kadabba were about the same size as modern chimps. Yet they were not forest apes. All three lived in areas where the rain forest had been replaced by a mixed habitat of woodlands, grasslands, and lakes. Small clues from their bones suggest that they might have moved around on two legs. Not as well as we do now, but definitely better than a modern chimp or bonobo. They could also still climb trees.

Sahel, Orrorin, and Kadabba also had something strange going on with their teeth. Their canine teeth were smaller than expected for apes of their size. Modern great apes use their canine teeth mostly for displays of aggression. This aggressive behavior is more common in males, whose canines are distinctly larger than those of females. The shrinking of Sahel, Orrorin, and Kadabba's mouth-daggers might mean an evolution toward more mellow behavior. This might be related to a need to stick together. After all, if there's safety in numbers, you probably shouldn't sink your teeth into your group-mate. But let's not hand out any Nobel Peace Prizes just yet. The other possibility is that Sahel, Orrorin, and Kadabba didn't need impressive canines to threaten rivals because they could stand upright and use their free hands to hurl stones.

Unfortunately we know very little about Sahel, Orrorin, and Kadabba because so few of their bones have been found. As scientists like to point out, understanding our species' history through fossils is like trying to figure out a complex movie plot based on just a few screenshots.

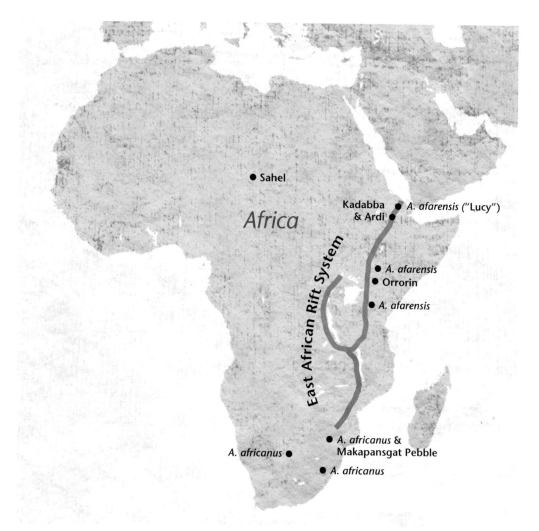

Sites where Sahelanthropus tchadensis *(Sahel)*, Orrorin tugenensis *(Orrorin)*,
Ardipithecus kadabba *(Kadabba)*, Ardipithecus ramidus *(Ardi)*, Australopithecus
afarensis *(Lucy's species), and* Australopithecus africanus *have been found.*

Around 4.5 million years ago, we get another screenshot: Ardi. Scientists have found the fossilized bones of several dozen individuals of Ardi's
species (*Ardipithecus ramidus*). Ardi was small—around 120 centimeters (4
feet) tall. It lived in a mixed habitat of woodlands and forest patches and
possibly added tubers (edible roots) to a chimp-like diet of fruit, nuts,
seeds, grubs, and honey. Ardi's long arm bones; long, curved finger bones;

and grasping big toe suggest that some part of Ardi's life was spent grabbing and swinging from branches. Yet Ardi did not have the same sort of wrist and hand as modern knuckle-walkers like chimps and gorillas. Based on its spine, leg, foot, and pelvis bones, Ardi could also move upright on the ground. Ardi wasn't yet an efficient walker or runner, though. Efficient walking requires angled thigh bones, a flexible foot, and a broad pelvis. Ardi was only partway there.

Remember: natural selection works upon whatever is around. A trait doesn't have to be perfect or optimal to be passed on. It just has to be a little bit better than what came before. If evolution had a motto, it would be *Yeah. Good Enough.*

Ardi's body wasn't yet optimal for upright walking.[2] But 4.5 million years ago, Ardi was good enough.

About a hundred thousand years after Ardi, the Australopiths arrived on the scene. They were possibly Ardi's descendants. The evolution of the Australopiths is a *"TA-DA!"* moment in human evolution. Scientists aren't sure if we're descended from Sahel, Orrorin, Kadabba, or Ardi. Our direct ancestors could have been another yet-undiscovered species. With the Australopiths it's a different story. There were at least six different species of Australopith, and they were around for about 2 million years. Their fossilized remains have been found in eastern, north-central, and southern Africa. One of these Australopith species is probably our direct ancestor (going back about 300,000 generations).

Modern Africa, with its wonderful diversity of animals, pales in comparison to the lost world of the Australopiths. They lived among saber-toothed cats, lions, leopards, and long-legged hunting hyenas. There were pigs the size of buffalos, three-hundred-pound baboons,

2   Don't get smug—our bodies aren't optimal, either. That's why so many people have back problems.

short-necked giraffes crowned with moose-like antlers, and short-trunked elephants that looked as if someone had pulled out their tusks and stuck them back in upside down.

Australopithecus afarensis lived about 3.7 to 3 million years ago. One particular find, a 3.2-million-year-old fossil from the northern edge of East Africa's rift valleys, rocked the scientific world when it was discovered. Most scientists would be overjoyed to find a handful of bones from such an ancient creature. This skeleton, nicknamed "Lucy," was 40 percent complete.

Like Ardi, Lucy was only three to four feet tall. Judging by her long arms and curved finger bones, she was still a good tree climber. Her kind probably foraged in trees and retreated into trees at night for safety. The fear of being attacked by a predator—of something lunging from the darkness—is still with us. It's the same terror that underlies horror movies.

A family of Australopithecus afarensis *(Lucy's species).*

Based on the differences in their feet, ankles, knees, and hips, Lucy was a better upright walker than Ardi. Ardi had a chimp-like foot with a grasping big toe, but Lucy's toes faced forward like ours. And Lucy's thigh bones, like those of modern humans, angled inward toward her knee. Angled thighs allow for more efficient walking. When each leg is closer to the center of our body, we can easily place all our weight on one leg at a time. Forest apes like chimps can't do this because their thigh bones aren't angled inward. To walk upright they must waddle awkwardly, shifting their weight from side to side. Australopiths like Lucy didn't walk like chimps; they walked in a near-human way.

Remarkably, we have footprints to prove it. About 3.7 million years ago, a volcano in Tanzania (East Africa) spewed ash across a valley. Three two-legged apes of different sizes walked through rain-soaked ash that later hardened into rock. Maybe the walkers were of Lucy's kind, or perhaps they were a different species of Australopith. But whoever walked through that ancient muck had a stride similar to ours. Their footprints, like human footprints, are close together along the line of travel, and parts of the sole of the foot sink deeper than other parts as the foot presses down and pushes off again. One walker's prints sank in slightly

3.7-million-year-old footprints from Laetoli, Tanzania (East Africa).

deeper on one side than the other, as if it were carrying extra weight on one hip. Could the walker have been toting a baby?

So the Australopiths walked upright. What was going on inside their heads?

Around 3.5 million years had passed since some knuckle-walking forest apes evolved into upright-walking apes of the woodlands, wetlands, and grasslands. Their bones, muscles, and ligaments had changed; they could walk farther with less effort in their search for food. But their brains were still about the same size. Based on skull volume, the brain of an Australopith was approximately 450 cubic centimeters (cc)—about the size of a modern chimp's. A modern human's brain is around three times larger (1,350 cc). At this point, based on brain-to-body ratios, ancient dolphins would have outranked our ancestors in the smarts department.

The Australopiths didn't have anything close to human language. Based on evidence from their skeletons, they didn't have the right kind of throats for making tiny variations in sound as they exhaled. Australopiths probably communicated as chimps do: with hoots, grunts, screams, and simple gestures. They surely used chimp-like alarm calls because there were plenty of predators to be alarmed about. As if giant hyenas and big saber-toothed cats weren't terrifying enough, the Australopiths also had to keep an eye on the sky. Judging by the talon marks gouged into the fossilized skull of a young Australopith known as the "Taung Child," it is clear that an African eagle had seized it by the head.

These ever-present dangers would've encouraged Australopiths to stick together. As social animals, they knew who belonged to their group and who was a stranger. We can imagine they recognized close kin—their mothers and maternal siblings. Chimps and bonobos don't form long-term bonds with their mating partners; it's likely Australopiths didn't, either.

The Makapansgat Pebble. Turn the book upside down and you'll see a slightly different face.

When two neighboring bands of Australopiths met, they may have interacted peacefully—or not so peacefully, depending on the circumstances. After all, if you recognize that certain individuals belong to your "in-group," that means other individuals must be the "out-group." Outsiders may not be welcome at your fig tree or your warthog carcass.

Did Australopiths feel affection for their band members? Did they share food or help the sick or injured? Did they wonder or imagine? We can't know for sure. The Australopiths weren't us. They were more like two-legged chimpanzees.

And yet . . .

A cluster of *Australopithecus africanus* fossils was found in Makapansgat Valley in South Africa. In the same layer as the bones, scientists discovered a lustrous red-brown rock now known as the Makapansgat Pebble. The pebble fits nicely into the palm of a hand. It's a completely natural object shaped by erosion and shows no marks of having been used as a tool. The closest source for this type of stone (jasperite) is several kilometers away. An Australopith must have noticed the pebble, picked it up, and carried it to where scientists uncovered it 3 million years later. Did that Australopith see what we see?

The Australopiths were not human. Yet this pebble whispers of what they might become.

A female Australopithecus afarensis *(Lucy).*

STEP 2
WE SMASH ROCKS

Bees circle a cavity in a tree. You start to drool.

Honey.

You find a baseball-bat-shaped piece of wood on the forest floor. A few swings break the beehive's protective wax plug. You grab a sturdy stick to pry the hive open, but the good stuff is still down deep. Hmm. You snatch a skinny stick for probing and scraping. Quick! The bees are swarming angrily. You pull out your honeycomb-clotted stick and sprint off. Sweet success!

Or . . .

You're so, so hungry. You've found a fat grub in a deep crack in a rotting log. But how to get it? Nearby there's a pandanus shrub with broad leaves edged by tiny barbs. Hmm. Maybe if you tear a leaf so it's thick at one end for gripping and thin at the other for probing, you could poke it in the crack. But the leaf has fibers running lengthwise. You can't tear it diagonally. So you tear across, then down, then across and down again. You now have a tool shaped like a long staircase that's thick at one end and narrow at the other. The grub is snagged and dragged out. Success!

In neither situation are you a human. In the first case you're a West African chimpanzee. In the second you're a New Caledonian crow.

Tool use seems to define humanity. This morning I used five tools (bowl, fork, pan, spatula, and stove) to scramble an egg. But we humans aren't the only tool-users. We also aren't the only species that uses multiple tools, one after the other, to achieve a goal. That honey-seeking chimp used a series of tools to break open the beehive. We aren't the only species that uses two tools simultaneously, either. Some chimps crack nuts by using a flat stone as an anvil and a rounder stone as a hammer. And we aren't the only species that takes a simple tool and improves it. New Caledonian crows use their beaks to whittle hooks into the end of sticks, and some chimps gnaw the end of sticks into sharp points to probe tree hollows for bush babies (small nocturnal primates as adorable as their name implies).

So there's plenty of tool using and toolmaking elsewhere in the animal kingdom. But there's still one kind of tool behavior that appears unique to humans and our direct ancestors: using a tool to make another tool. Along with upright walking, this ability is the foundation of humanity.

A wild New Caledonian crow with a stick tool.

As you may recall, about 3 million years ago, our Australopith ancestors were using their bizarre two-leggedness to move around the varied landscapes of eastern and southern Africa. Though we don't know for sure, it's reasonable to assume that at least some Australopiths used simple tools. Perhaps stones for crushing nuts, grass stems for termite-fishing, and sticks for gathering honey and digging tubers out of the ground. Our evolutionary cousins the chimps do all of these things, and we know Australopiths had chimp-sized brains. Australopiths may have used tools more often than modern chimps since they were upright walkers and had free hands.

So tools were useful for filling the belly with nuts, termites, honey, and tubers. There was also a lot of meat walking around the rift valleys.

Scientists have discovered cut marks on 3.4-million-year-old antelope and wild-cattle bones in Ethiopia (East Africa). It looks as if meat had been sliced off with a sharp-edged stone. The only hominin known to live in that area at that time was an Australopith of Lucy's species: *Australopithecus afarensis*. ("Hominins" include humans and all the other species descended from those upright-walking forest apes.)

In another part of the East African Rift System, scientists found 3.3-million-year-old stones with a cutting edge. Somebody had struck one rock (a hammerstone) against another to knock off a sharp shard.

I know what you're thinking. A broken rock—what's the big deal? But stick with me.

Using a tool (a rock) to make another tool (a sharp-edged flake) is one tool behavior that only we humans and our two-legged ancestors are known to do. Around 3 million years ago, it was the highest of high tech. This brilliant innovation gave our ancestors a new way to fill their stomachs.

In the 1960s the legendary field biologist George Schaller decided to test how our early ancestors might have survived on the African savanna.

He and a friend took a series of hikes, always unarmed, through a game park.[1] Besides small animals like frogs and nestling birds, they came across several dead gazelles with meat still on the bones. They watched a cheetah kill an antelope fawn—meat they could have stolen by driving off the cat. Later, a group of vultures lounging in a tree alerted them to the remains of a zebra killed by a lion. Though only the skeleton was left, George and his friend used a sharp-edged stone to smash the leg bones, exposing the nutritious bone marrow inside. "And with the same tool I bashed in the back of the skull, exposing the brain, potentially a nice snack," George wrote cheerfully.

During their walks, George and his friend also found a sick zebra foal and a blind baby giraffe. Human ancestors, they guessed, could've killed such vulnerable animals by bludgeoning them with clubs or stones.

Imagine you're a member of a small band of Australopiths. Maybe you've killed some unlucky zebra foal or baby giraffe. It's only a matter of time before hyenas, lions, and saber-toothed cats invite themselves over for dinner and decide *you're* the appetizer. What to do?

Instead of just wolfing down whatever you can tear off with your puny teeth—which are definitely not designed to slice zebra or giraffe hide—you use your sharp-edged stone tool to chop the carcass into smaller chunks. You and your fellow Australopiths sprint off to a cluster of nearby trees with your hunks of bloody zebra, dragging your dinner along as you climb to safety.

Think of this as the origin of takeout.

Perhaps not all Australopiths made flaked tools. Maybe some didn't have the necessary hard-but-brittle stones nearby. But some Australopiths discovered that certain kinds of rocks will fracture if hit at just the right angle. That first sharp-edged tool might have been a lucky accident.

---

1   Do not try this.

In ancient stone toolmaking, a lumpy hammerstone was used to knock a sharp-edged flake off a core stone. Flakes and core stones could be used for scraping or chopping. The very earliest stone tools from 3.3 million years ago are called "Lomekwian" after the place in Kenya (East Africa) where they were discovered.

An Australopith trying to smash a nut breaks her hammerstone. She picks up the flake . . . a light bulb goes on . . . and the rest is prehistory.

Butchering carcasses was a great leap forward. But sharp-edged tools had additional advantages. Some modern chimps use sticks to dig up tubers, so it's reasonable to assume Australopiths did, too. An Australopith might have improved their digging stick by using an edged stone to carve the tip into a point or a spade shape.

With a sharp-edged stone, you can also smash and tenderize raw meat and raw tubers, making them easier to chew and digest.[2] Smashing and grinding may have been particularly important for the survival of young children, who lacked the jaw power to chow down on raw warthog.

---

2   I considered experimenting on myself by timing how long it took to me to chew and swallow equal weights of (1) raw meat, (2) raw meat smashed with a stone dredged from my backyard, and (3) cooked meat. But though I'm devoted to you, dear reader, I decided I'm just not *that* devoted.

A female Homo habilis *(Handy Person).*

Yes, our ancestors made tools. But tools also made our ancestors.

If you're an Australopith who is better at making and using tools than other Australopiths, you're going to find it easier to get the calories you need to survive. If you have superior tool skills, you're likely to eat more meat—an especially nutritious food—than an Australopith who's all thumbs. And if you're also better at passing your stone-using and stone-flaking techniques to your offspring, you've hit the jackpot.

If the environment consistently selects for Australopiths who are better at making tools, using tools, and passing on tool skills, those traits will spread through the Australopith population. Maybe the trait being selected is a type of hand that allows a better grip. Maybe the trait is better hand-eye coordination. Maybe the trait is a behavior, like being more tolerant of curious children who want to imitate toolmaking. If enough time passes and enough traits change, you end up with a population that is no longer quite as Australopith-y as before. A new species has evolved.

About 2.4 million years ago, we find the first evidence of a new species, *Homo habilis* ("Handy Man"). Handy People have the distinction of being the first official member of the *Homo* clan, of which we humans (*Homo sapiens*) are the only surviving species. But it's more accurate to think of the Handy People as a shiny new model of Australopith. They were about the same size as Australopiths—about four feet tall—with slightly longer legs. But their name fits. Where scientists find Handy People fossils, they often find stone tools.

Given that their species name translates as "Handy Man," you might get the impression that making and using tools was a male-dominated activity. That's probably wrong. Among modern chimps, females are more skillful with tools than males. And stone tools have so many uses—mashing tubers, cracking bones, smashing dead wood to get at grubs—

that every adult Handy Person, male or female, probably needed some amount of tool skill to survive.

Handy People used stones as choppers, scrapers, and pounders. Their simple technology is called the "Oldowan" after Olduvai Gorge in East Africa (Tanzania), where the first Handy People fossils were discovered, along with tools and animal bones. It seems Handy People actively hunted smaller, younger animals, like baby gazelles, while scavenging the carcasses of larger, dangerous animals, like giant pigs, hippos, and elephants.

Handy People weren't the only hominins living in Africa. There were still different kinds of Australopiths around, including several species known as "robust Australopiths" for their heavy jaws and teeth.

But wait . . . didn't Australopiths evolve into Handy People?

Evolution is a journey, not a destination. It produces different outcomes in different places because different environments select for different traits. The rift system that runs through eastern and southern Africa stretches for thousands of kilometers across an immense continent. In particularly challenging areas of the rift, perhaps only the best tool-users survived. One of those challenging, difficult-to-survive places may have produced the Handy People. Heavy-jawed, robust Australopiths may have been more common in places that had reliable supplies of fruit, nuts, and seedpods but less big game. As far as we know, robust Australopiths didn't make sharp-edged stone tools for cutting meat from carcasses.

Maybe there were multiple hominin species around 2.4 million years ago because there were multiple answers to the question: What sort of hominin can survive in the varied landscape of eastern and southern Africa?

Handy People were a significant step up, brain-wise, from the Australopiths. Based on the size of their skulls, the brains of Australopiths were still chimp-sized (450 cc). Handy People's brains were around 610 cc.

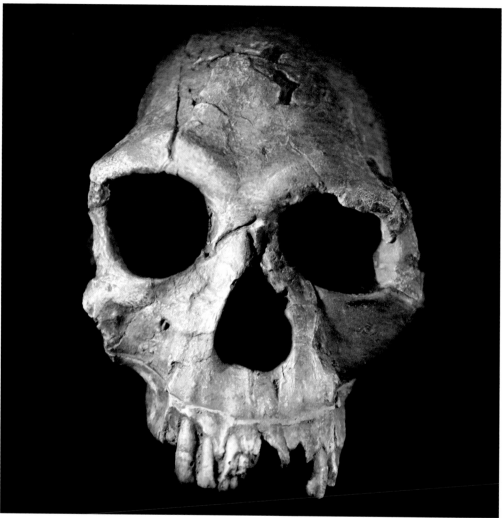

The 1.8-million-year-old skull of a Homo habilis *(Handy Person).*

If an alien zookeeper hunting for Earth's brainiest animal landed here around 2 million years ago, would that alien pick a Handy Person? Sorry, no. Based on brain-to-body-weight ratios, dolphins would still come out on top. But the gap was closing.

What drove the increase in Handy People's braininess? Toolmaking, for starters. To manufacture an Oldowan-style tool requires intelligence, memory, and fine motor skills. You must choose the correct material and strike with just the right amount of force at the perfect angle—while avoiding smashing your fingers.[3]

Scientists believe extractive foraging (which includes tool using) is one of the two main drivers in the evolution of intelligence. The other driver is social life.

The environment tests and the environment selects obviously applies to the physical environment (the climate, the kind of food available, etc.). But if you're an animal that lives in groups, your social environment also tests and selects. It's no coincidence all of the species considered highly intelligent (crows, ravens, parrots, dolphins, whales, elephants, monkeys, and apes) are extractive foragers living in social groups.

Our ancestors surely foraged together to keep from being picked off by predators. Handy People may also have used home bases, judging by the piles of cut-marked bones and stone tools scientists have found concentrated in small areas. A defensible base (perhaps a cluster of rocks) would make it easier to drive off any saber-tooth or hyena that came nosing around. A base might also mean Handy People shared food.

We don't find anything remarkable about people gathering for dinner and passing the turkey. But sharing food isn't common among our closest relatives. About the only time chimps share food is after a successful monkey hunt. Despite hunting in a group, chimps don't seem to have a coordinated strategy; it's every chimp for himself or herself. (Both males and females hunt, though males usually make the kill.) The chimp that kills the monkey will sometimes dole out scraps to chimps that come begging. But sharing is much more likely if the monkey-killer and the beggar have a strong social bond.

---

3   Two million years ago is still too early for real language. But I like to imagine that an injured thumb during stone-flaking triggered the world's first swear word.

If Handy People regularly returned to a home base with whatever they foraged, killed, or scavenged, it's reasonable to assume they shared their goodies (at least sometimes). It's also reasonable to assume Handy People shared as a way of cementing social bonds. Bonds might be based on family relationships, alliances, who you had mated with, or who you hoped to mate with. It's possible that a handful of cracked nuts was like a friendship bracelet. A raw hippo kidney showed you really cared.

Sharing is also a survival strategy. Many modern hunter-gatherer societies get the majority of their day-to-day calories from plant foods like seeds and tubers. Meat is important, but hunters might often come home empty-handed. If those who hunt and those who gather cooperate by sharing food, everyone is better off.

Of course, effective sharing requires that you remember others and your past interactions with them: *I'm giving you antelope liver today because yesterday you gave me mashed tubers.* Handy People with social smarts—those who were better at forming bonds and sharing food—were more likely to survive lean times. They were more likely to leave behind descendants that inherited their parents' savvy.

Cooperation was also our ancestors' best defense against predators. Two million years ago Handy People, not to mention the remaining Australopiths, were definitely not at the top of the food chain. One Handy Person's fossilized foot bones bear the gouges of crocodile teeth. And judging by the distinctive punctures left in the skull of a robust Australopith, it was ambushed from behind by a leopard. The cat sank its upper canines into the eye sockets and its lower canines into the back of the Australopith's head.

A single Handy Person or Australopith was always vulnerable. But just as a dive-bombing, shrieking flock of crows can send a hawk into

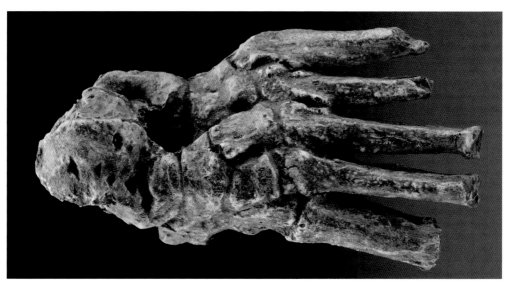

A cast of a fossilized Homo habilis *(Handy Person) foot. The holes in the ankle bone were made by crocodile teeth.*

retreat, a large-enough group of howling, stone-throwing hominins could fend off even a saber-tooth. The more closely the hominins cooperated by keeping lookout and mounting a defense, the more likely it was that the individuals in the group would survive.

Of course, there are always those who try to do less than their fair share. Cooperation breaks down if cheaters get away with cheating. For cooperation to work, there needs to be some basic sense of fairness shared by everyone in the group, an ability to identify cheaters, and a willingness to take action against them. These social skills require brainpower.

We know very little about how Handy People communicated. But given their bigger brains, they were probably better at expressing themselves than Australopiths. Handy People likely used more sounds, more gestures, and more combinations of the two. Slackers no doubt got the message when they didn't do their part to drive off a leopard.[4]

---

4   Alternatively, they may have had a rock bounced off their skull by an indignant group-mate. Yet another use for hand-eye coordination.

No one knows if Handy People had a sclera (the white part of the eyeball). This may seem disconnected from how we communicate, but stay with me. Scientists think the sclera evolved to allow "gaze signaling." The contrast of bright white next to the darker iris and pupil allows us to easily direct another person's attention to where we are looking. The whites of our eyes also make our faces more expressive.

We don't know which hominin was the first to have white eyeballs. But at some point in our evolution, someone did something wrong . . . and someone else invented the eye roll.

Let's take stock of the situation 2 million years ago. We're still menu items for big predators. We're still getting chased down and gobbled up. But we're fully upright. Our brains are larger, and we're cooperating more. We're knocking stones together and making a variety of simple tools. Those tools may lack touch screens, wheels, and even handles, but they are the foundation upon which all future technology will be built.

When you wake up tomorrow and shuffle into the bathroom, start a list of every tool you use. (A tool is an unattached object used to manipulate something else.) Your hairbrush is a tool. So is your toothbrush. The toothpaste isn't, but the toothpaste tube is . . .

I suspect you'll throw in the towel before you hit fifty. No worries. Just consider: Every tool you use is a gift. A gift passed to you without fail, hand to hand across millions of years and hundreds of thousands of generations. A gift tracing all the way back to the calloused, dirt-stained palms of Australopiths and Handy People.

And along with these gifts came another: the big bulbous thing sitting on top of your neck, cradled inside your skull.

A female Homo erectus.

STEP 3
WE GET SWELLED HEADS

Our earliest ancestors needed intelligence to make and use tools. They also needed brainpower to navigate their social lives. By the time Handy People evolved, the line of two-legged apes that would eventually lead to us had existed for about 4.5 million years. Yet the brain of a Handy Person was still only about half the size of a modern human's.

If an extra-large brain is an extra-large advantage, why did it take so long to evolve?

First of all, large brains are costly. Although the modern human brain is only about 2 percent of our body weight, it uses 20 to 25 percent of our energy. It's like having a gas-guzzling Ferrari inside your skull.

Without a calorie-rich diet, a large brain can't even *begin* to evolve. We're fortunate that the scavenging talents of our earliest ancestors delivered the high-quality food that made our big brains possible.[1] We're also lucky a shifting climate made it difficult—probably brutally difficult—for our ancestors to survive. This doesn't sound lucky, but it was.

We know about these climate swings because past climates leave their mark upon the Earth. Those marks linger in gases trapped in Arctic ice, in tree rings, in sediments, and in fossilized plants and animals. Scientists

---

1   In addition to raw meat, scavenging added treats like raw bone marrow, raw guts, and raw brains to the menu. Bon appétit.

know that between 2.1 and 1.7 million years ago, the climate kept flip-flopping back and forth between wet and dry. Lakes filled, shrank, dried up, and refilled. Woodlands turned to arid grasslands and back again. This wasn't something that happened in a single hominin's lifetime. Yet by the timescale of evolution, the changes were rapid. Whole communities of plants and animals were affected. Populations that couldn't adapt quickly enough went extinct.

Our ancestors were already smart and flexible. The seesawing climate probably selected individuals who were even cleverer and more versatile. The ones handiest with tools. Those who could solve problems and innovate. The individuals who could best remember where to find food and water in different situations. The fig trees are withered? Search the branches for a dead gazelle stashed there by a leopard. There's a fish flopping in a drying-up pond? Use a digging stick to kill it. The grass is dead? Dig in the sand for tubers, and carry them with you as you search for a better place to live.

This wasn't the first time hominins had to deal with an erratic climate. Lucy's kind (*Australopithecus afarensis*) evolved during an earlier period of climate instability around 3.7 million years ago. The climate was also shifting about 2.4 million years ago when Handy People first appeared. *The environment tests and the environment selects.* The climate instability around 2 million years ago coincides with the evolution of a radically new kind of hominin: *Homo erectus.*

Australopiths and Handy People can fairly be described as advanced two-legged apes. *Homo erectus* crossed the threshold into humanity. Erectus was human-sized with roughly human proportions, though stockier. If one were alive today, you might easily—at least from behind—mistake an Erectus for a modern human who did a lot of weight lifting. Only when she turned would you stumble backward in surprise. The size of her skull would suggest human-like intelligence, but her low sloping forehead and thick brow ridges would look very different from a modern human's.

The brains of Australopiths, as you may recall, averaged 450 cc. Drop a brain that size into a blender and the liquefied result would fill slightly less than two coffee cups. It took another 1.5 million years to reach Handy People's brain volume of 610 cc, a size that would fill 2.6 coffee cups. On average, that's adding two teaspoons of brain every 100,000 years.

Just 600,000 years later the brains of Erectus averaged 980 cc: a volume of about four coffee cups. That's an additional twelve teaspoons of brain every 100,000 years—six times faster than before. The rapidly shifting climate seems to have created a strong selection pressure for bigger brains. Smarts equaled survival.

Given this growth spurt, you might think: "Ah, we must finally be brainier than dolphins!" Nope. If alien scientists had visited Earth a million years ago and calculated the brain-to-body ratio for hominins versus dolphins, dolphins would still have had the advantage. But we were catching up.

Of course, the increase in Erectus's brain size wouldn't have happened if Erectus wasn't able to find enough food to fuel its bigger brain. Based on its larger body and larger brain, it's estimated the daily energy needs of an Erectus were 80 percent higher than those of an Australopith.

Erectus did many of the things Australopiths and Handy People did. Only better. Their long legs, sturdy joints, arched feet, short toes, and muscled rear ends[2] allowed them to walk and run more efficiently over long distances compared to Australopiths or Handy People. Ranging over a bigger area means you're more likely to find something to scavenge. And Erectus may have begun hunting medium-sized grazing animals by adopting the same technique as African wild dogs.

---

2   Yes, fossilized skeletons can tell us something about ancient butts. Just another wonder of science.

An animal's body can be adapted for sprinting or for sustained distance running, but it's difficult to be good at both. Many African antelopes, such as the Thomson's gazelle, evolved to outrun big cats and hyenas. They can sprint, but not for long. African wild dogs take advantage of this. Members of a pack take turns pursuing a gazelle, forcing it toward other dogs waiting to pick up the chase, until it collapses from exhaustion.

Compared to other African mammals, our Erectus ancestors were laughably slow. Yet they may have been the original marathoners, able to keep going kilometer after kilometer. Old, sick, injured, or young prey would've been particularly vulnerable to a determined band of hungry, relay-racing hominins.

This type of hunting isn't just a matter of physical fitness. It also takes intelligence. Our ancestors couldn't hunt by scent like most predators because they had a pathetic sense of smell. In place of a good nose, they used their brain. To find prey an Erectus hunting band had to read the landscape. They had to assess dozens of small clues like animal tracks and

An African wild dog on the chase.

animal droppings. After locating potential prey, they faced more decisions. How best to approach the prey? If in a herd, which animal to target?

The chase itself required close cooperation, a knowledge of everyone's strengths and weaknesses, and a way of getting heavy stone tools to the carcass quickly so it could be cut up before lions and hyenas arrived. Perhaps Erectus used a division of labor: this hunter is best at flushing game, and these hunters excel at the long chase, while the one carrying the tools follows behind the others, watching the pursuit from a distance and taking shortcuts whenever possible.

As you may remember, standing upright helped keep our ancestors from overheating because less of their body surface was directly exposed to the sun. Having sweat glands helped, too. It's also likely Erectus was less hairy than earlier hominins. Having less body hair made sweating more efficient and kept Erectus cool. An upright posture, sweating, and sparser hair allowed Erectus to chase their prey for many kilometers without keeling over from heatstroke.

Changes in body hair, by the way, may have driven a change in our skin color. Forest-living great apes like chimpanzees have brown faces, but the skin underneath their dark fur is pinkish white. Our early ancestors probably had similar fur and skin. As the environment selected individuals with less body hair, it also selected those with darker skin. Darker skin contains a chemical (melanin) that protects against sun damage. In other words, as we became less ape-like and more human-like, our skin darkened.

Much of what we know about Erectus comes from a fossil dubbed "Nariokotome Boy." When the boy died in a swamp in what is now Kenya (East Africa) about 1.6 million years ago, his body fell into the mud. He wasn't killed by a crocodile or a hippo. Based on marks on his jawbone, he likely suffered a lingering death from a gum infection.

Nariokotome Boy was tall—about 1.6 meters (5 feet, 3 inches). Though he had the frame of an adolescent, a microscopic exam of his teeth suggests he was only eight or nine years old when he died. (Tooth enamel is laid down daily, and by studying the enamel layers, scientists can tell how quickly an animal reaches adulthood.) Based on scientific analysis of Nariokotome Boy's teeth, Erectus children grew up twice as fast as human children. This is similar to the growth rates of chimps and bonobos.

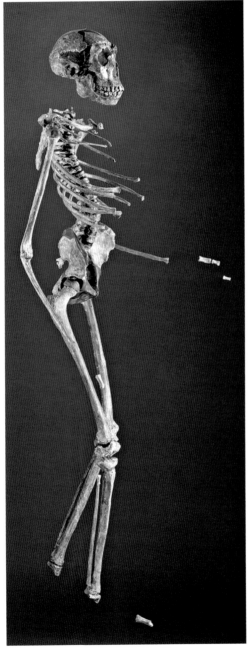

A cast of Nariokotome Boy's skeleton.

We don't know much about Nariokotome Boy's home life. How were the individuals in his group bonded to each other? Did males and females form strong family ties, or were other relationships more important? Did some individuals dominate? If there was a division of labor, who did the hunting and who did the gathering?

Scientists often look to chimps for clues to the social lives of our early human ancestors. Male chimps commonly form alliances with close relatives—fathers, brothers, and uncles. These buddy groups

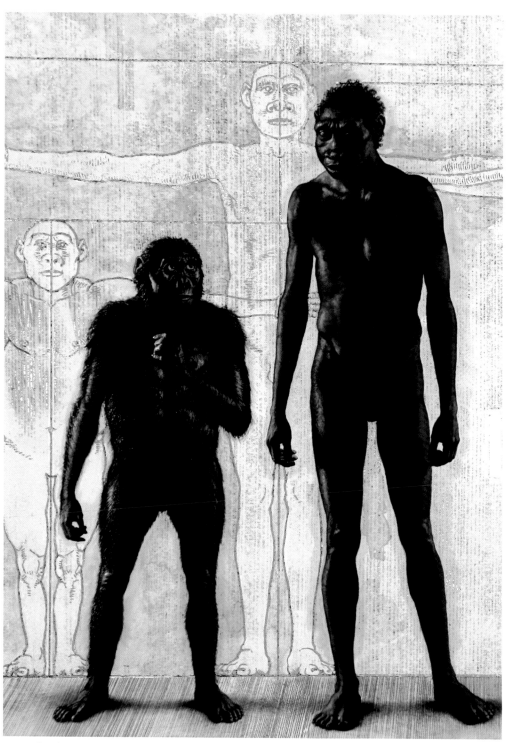

Lucy (left) and Nariokotome Boy (right).

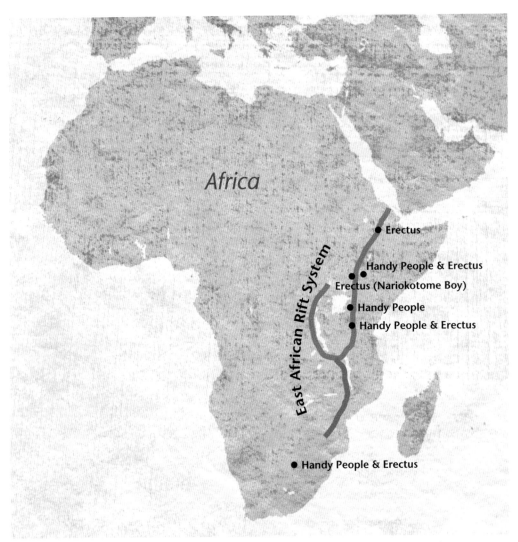

Sites where fossils of Homo habilis *(Handy People) and* Homo erectus *(Erectus) have been discovered.*

jostle for power and are dominant over females. Male chimps can be violently aggressive toward rivals, and chimps from one group may even join forces to attack and kill males from neighboring groups. The bonds between female chimps aren't as tight as the bonds between allied males, possibly because when female chimps grow up, they leave the group in which they were born and join another.

Yet we humans are just as closely related to bonobos as we are to chimps. Bonobos offer a very different way of thinking about how our ancestors might have lived. Though female bonobos, like female chimps, leave their birth group when they are sexually mature, female bonobos form tight friendships with other females in their new group. Male bonobos don't usually dominate females, and males remain close to their mothers throughout their life. Violence among bonobos is rare.

Modern human hunter-gatherer societies offer another model for the social lives of our ancestors. Of course, modern hunter-gatherers have been evolving for as long as any other group of humans. But since hunting and gathering is humanity's oldest way of making a living, scientists think modern hunter-gather societies may preserve other ancient traditions. In these societies male-female pair-bonding is the norm. And though a division of labor between men and women is also the norm, there are many variations. In some hunter-gatherer societies, male hunters supply most of the food. In others, women provide most of the calories by gathering plants and tubers. In some cultures women hunt. In others they don't. In some societies, when a woman is ready to find a mate, she leaves the group into which she was born and joins another. In other societies it's the man who leaves. Most modern hunter-gatherer groups, interestingly, are egalitarian rather than male dominated. Everybody usually has a say.

We all tend to think in patterns set by our own culture. It might seem right and natural to imagine an Erectus guy bringing back a buffalo foreleg buzzing with flies to his Erectus mate, who has spent her day scratching tubers out of the dirt while keeping their two kids from being snatched by hyenas. But we don't know what Erectus was doing a million and a half years ago. We can only explore the possibilities. It does seem likely close kin pitched in to help pregnant and breastfeeding females get the extra nutrition they needed to fuel the growth of their babies' big brains.

We do know those big-brained Erectus invented new and better tools.

The Oldowan tools made by Handy People and some Australopiths were relatively simple. Erectus, however, invented the Acheulean handaxe, named after the site where the first ones were discovered. With its tapered shape and sharp edges, the Acheulean handaxe was much better for butchering carcasses than Oldowan choppers and scrapers. To fashion a handaxe, the toolmaker struck a large oval flake off a stone and then shaped it by knocking smaller flakes off the edges on both sides. As the edges of the handaxe dulled from use, they could be reflaked.

If we judge the success of a design by how long it was used, the Acheulean handaxe is the all-time champ. It was our ancestors' tool of choice for a million years.

Yet a tool can be more than a tool. Most ancient handaxes are about the size of a human hand. Some, however, are so large they were impractical to use. One handaxe discovered in Algeria (North Africa) is 35 centimeters (14 inches long). It's too big and heavy to wield one-handed like a normal handaxe. Knocking this behemoth off a boulder and chipping it into a pleasing teardrop shape required both strength and skill. Was its creator less interested in making a handy handaxe than in making a statement? If the answer is yes, you're looking at one of our first sculptures.[3]

Right about now you may be wondering: What happened to Australopiths and Handy People when Erectus showed up?

Africa 2 million years ago was home to a diverse group of hominins. At least three species of Australopiths lingered, along with two varieties of Handy People. As you may recall, just because one species evolves from

---

3   Made by one of our first show-offs?

another doesn't necessarily mean the first species goes extinct. A population living in a stable environment may not change much, while a population living in a different area may face such strong selection pressure that a new species evolves. (Scientists call this process "speciation.")

A supersized handaxe from Algeria (North Africa).

Two million years ago Erectus was the big new kid on the block. As Erectus bands spread across eastern and southern Africa, they likely came into contact with Australopiths and Handy People.

Though we don't know how everybody got along, we can use modern great apes as a model. Of the four living species of nonhuman great apes (chimps, bonobos, gorillas, and orangutans), only chimps and gorillas cross paths in the wild. Sometimes chimps and gorillas feed within sight of each other without any drama. Sometimes chimps throw a fit, screaming and slapping branches, if gorillas approach a fruit tree the chimps feel they already have dibs on. Gorillas aren't as aggressive as chimps, but given a gorilla's superior size and strength, it can do pretty much anything it wants.

When Australopiths, Handy People, and Erectus encountered each other, there may have been a whole range of different reactions, depending on how many individuals were on each side, whether food was at stake,

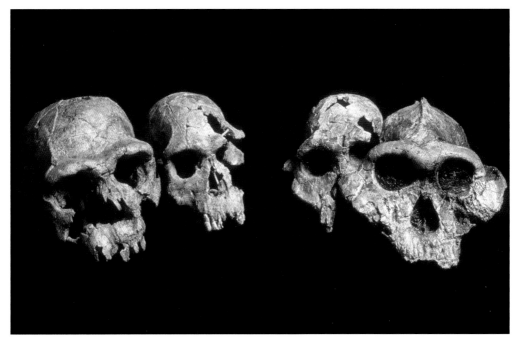

A collection of 1.5-million-year-old fossil skulls, all found in the same geological layer in Tanzania (East Africa). From left to right: an Erectus, a Handy Person, a female robust Australopith, and a male robust Australopith.

and who was hungrier. In an aggressive encounter over a valuable carcass, it's easy to imagine bigger-bodied, bigger-brained Erectus seizing the prize. Hominins killing and eating each other can't be ruled out. But avoidance or some level of uneasy coexistence may have been the norm.

It's also possible hominins of different species occasionally mated and gave birth to a hybrid youngster. Hybridization between closely related species isn't common in the wild, but it happens.[4]

Does the idea of a hybrid hominin sound far-fetched? Consider this: it's likely nobody alive is 100 percent pure *Homo sapiens*. (More on that later.)

---

4   For example, present-day climate change is bringing wild grizzly bears and wild polar bears into contact. Their half-and-half offspring are often a blush color, as if deeply embarrassed by being dubbed "pizzly" bears.

Eventually some of Africa's hominins headed north. Erectus for certain; perhaps others. These pioneers may have been drawn in that direction by herds of grazing animals seeking better pastures. Perhaps the landscape turned arid and they were forced to move as food sources dwindled. However it happened, some enterprising hominins wandered north, possibly along the Nile. Then they turned right.

There have been many notable adventurers over the millennia, including the first modern humans to reach Asia, Australia, Europe, the Americas, and the islands of Oceania. Yet the greatest exploration of all time belongs to barefoot bands of ancient ancestors. They left our mother continent behind, boldly going where no hominin had gone before.

Nariokotome Boy.

STEP 4
WE TAKE A HIKE

This is going to seem wildly off-topic. But for a moment let's consider Japanese, the language with the world's most complex writing system.

Children in Japan must learn two different syllable-based systems, each with 142 symbols. Then they must learn about 1,800 characters adopted from the Chinese writing system. Many of these characters have multiple meanings and pronunciations depending on how they are being used.

What did an Erectus like Nariokotome Boy need to know?

Today's East African savanna is home to over one thousand different species of birds, mammals, reptiles, and amphibians, plus dozens of species of edible plants and insects. And that's a low estimate. In Nariokotome Boy's time East Africa probably had more species than it does today.

Each animal species has its own behaviors. Many food items are found in different places at different times of the year. If you have the brainpower to absorb and remember countless small details about everything from gazelles to grubs, you're more likely to survive the lean times. Especially when you're living long before the invention of spears, bows and arrows, nets, fishhooks, snares, slings, and blowguns.

Let's say you want to hunt fledgling birds. Fledglings, unlike adults, are awkward and naive. A fledgling is vulnerable to being knocked out of a tree by a well-aimed stone. Can you recognize a fledgling's begging call as it asks its parent to feed it? If so, you can zero in on the fledgling and hurl your stone.

But wait. Adults of that species also make a begging call, asking their mate to bring them food as they sit on their eggs. Can you recognize that call? It sounds slightly different from a fledgling's call. The adult's call gives away the location of a nest. You can climb up and gather the eggs. The catch is that every bird species has its own set of calls. If you want to be an effective hunter of fledglings and gatherer of eggs, you need to carry an encyclopedia of bird sounds around in your head. Otherwise, you would waste time and energy flinging stones at adult birds too wary to ever be struck, or climbing trees without finding a single egg. Even if you occasionally found food by sheer luck, you'd slowly starve. The effort of random searching would use up more energy than you would get from the paltry bits of food you stumbled across.

This is not to say Erectus ate *every* kind of animal on the savanna. Some animals ate Erectus. And many of the larger plant-eaters were dangerous, too. If you hoped to keep breathing, you needed an intimate knowledge of all the scary animals sharing your neighborhood. When is a hippo most likely to crush you into a pulp?[1] What do you do if you're charged by an angry ostrich and there's no tree to climb?[2] If you're fleeing a rampaging elephant, should you confuse your pursuer by dashing through a pride of lions?[3] Africa is also home to plenty of small deadly creatures: poisonous snakes, spiders, and scorpions. Knowing how to avoid them extended your life.

---

1   When you block its path back to the water.

2   Lie facedown on the ground. Ostriches slash downward with the heavy claw on their middle toe. An ostrich can disembowel you with this *Karate Kid* move, but if you're lying flat on your stomach, it can only stomp on your head.

3   No idea. If you try this, let me know how things turn out.

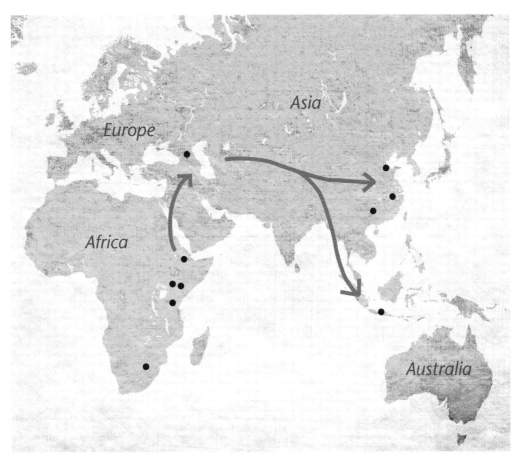

Fossils and stone tools (marked with dots) are evidence of **Homo** erectus's *migration out of Africa, through eastern Europe, and into mainland Asia and Southeast Asia. Modern coastlines are shown for clarity.*

Memorizing 1,800 Chinese characters doesn't seem so tough now, does it?

When groups of Erectus left Africa, they took along their ability to learn about their environment. They applied their skills to every ecosystem they encountered. Generation by generation they spread north and east. By 1.8 million years ago, they had reached eastern Europe, and by 1.7 million years ago, they had reached China. By 1.5 million years ago, Erectus was living in tropical Southeast Asia. To make these migrations

Erectus had to learn to live in forests, grasslands, and arid places very different from those in Africa.

Here's something intriguing, though. There are hints that maybe Erectus wasn't the only hominin to wander the world.

Scientists recently discovered stone tools in China near the remains of wild cattle, pigs, and deer. The tools are 2.1 million years old. That's earlier than the earliest fossils of Erectus. Who made the tools? Perhaps Erectus evolved earlier than we think and left Africa earlier, too. Or maybe another hominin left home before Erectus.

Which brings us to the "Hobbits."

The fossils of two new hominin species were recently discovered on two different islands in Southeast Asia. Because of the fossils' short stature—around 1.1 meters (3.6 feet) tall—scientists nicknamed these species "Hobbits." Are the Hobbits downsized versions of Erectus? Or are they descendants of Handy People—or even Australopiths—who left Africa long before Erectus? No Australopith or Handy Person fossil has ever been found outside Africa, but maybe evidence is out there waiting to be discovered.

You'll hear more about Hobbits later. Now let's turn to Wookiees.

If any Erectus left Africa hoping to find a safer neighborhood, they were sorely disappointed. In those days Asia, like Africa, was home to saber-tooths, lions, leopards, hyenas, elephants, and rhinos. But Asia also had bears, tigers, and a great ape that makes every other ape look not-so-great by comparison.

Gigantopithecus blacki looked like a gigantic Wookiee. It may have stood as much as ten feet tall and may have weighed 500 kilograms (1,100 pounds). If so, that's about three times bigger than the biggest gorilla—and almost three feet taller than Chewbacca. At least this gargantuan ape was a plant-eater. Still, you wouldn't want to give it any reason to dislike you.

A female Homo floresiensis *(Flores Hobbit).*

Erectus survived in new habitats alongside Wookiees and lions and tigers and bears[4] because their big brains gave them the ability to learn and adapt. They also developed tools that helped them exploit their new environments.

We know Erectus used stone tools. Scientists think they made tools from other materials as well. Erectus bands living in Asia surely noticed bamboo. Bamboo is light and sturdy, holds a sharp edge, and grows in hollow sections. If cut at the right spot, bamboo can be used as a container for food or water.

Erectus all over the world likely invented tools made of plant matter: digging sticks, dried gourds for storing water, shelters or barricades of branches and thorny bushes to keep safe at night, wood or bamboo rafts for crossing water, and vines dried into cords for tying things. Unfortunately, we'll never know for certain. All of it decomposed long ago.

Some Erectus living in Southeast Asia invented shell tools. About 500,000 years ago, on the island of Java in Indonesia, a sharpened freshwater mussel shell was crafted into a knife-like blade. At the same site, scientists discovered the first known engraving: a simple zigzag pattern scratched onto a mussel shell. It appears purely decorative. Was an Erectus seized by the same urge that causes us to doodle in notebooks?

So Erectus had the brains to remember crucial information about plants and animals, to make different kinds of tools, and maybe even to create our first art. But an Erectus like Nariokotome Boy didn't have to figure out all this on his own. It's likely that by the time of Erectus—if not before—our ancestors were passing survival skills to youngsters through a technique that connects individual brains. It's called teaching.

---

4   Oh my.

A mussel shell from Indonesia (Southeast Asia), decorated by Erectus about 500,000 years ago.

Teaching is a way of pooling knowledge and benefiting from other people's experiences. Through teaching, we speed up the learning of essential information. Through teaching, we avoid constantly reinventing the wheel.[5]

Teaching is surprisingly rare in nature. The scientific definition of teaching is strict: the teacher must vary their behavior in a way that benefits the learner but costs the teacher. For example, a mother cheetah may give her cubs a young gazelle she has injured—but not killed—so the cubs can learn how to dispatch prey. If the mother cheetah killed the gazelle outright, she would have a better chance of eating because cheetah kills are often stolen by hyenas and lions. Instead, she sacrifices so her cubs can learn gazelle-killing.

Adult killer whales will sometimes fling a captured sea lion toward a

---

5   Although from Erectus's point of view, the wheel is as futuristic as the *Millennium Falcon*.

nearby juvenile, despite the risk of the sea lion escaping. And adult meerkats will bite the stinger off a scorpion so youngsters can practice killing the scorpion without the danger of being stung.

You might think super-smart, tool-using species—chimps, New Caledonian crows, and bottlenose dolphins—would actively teach their young. That doesn't seem to be the case. Young chimps mostly learn how to crack a nut with a hammerstone and anvil by watching their mothers. Once in a while a mother chimp will reposition a stone for a juvenile, but that's about it. Young New Caledonian crows appear to learn how to make and use tools by closely observing their parents and playing with their parents' discarded tools. Some bottlenose dolphins use sponges to protect their noses as they search the seafloor for hidden fish, but the mother dolphin doesn't seem to do any active teaching. Her calf watches and imitates.

This wild bottlenose dolphin uses a sponge on her rostrum (snout) to protect it from getting scraped when she noses around on the seafloor for fish hiding on the bottom. Dolphins become "spongers" only if they have spent several years watching their mother use sponge tools.

Teaching may be rare among other species, but it is universal in human societies. We are particularly good at teaching because we're good communicators. It's possible the need to teach, and the need to learn, drove us to communicate more—and better.

Let's imagine there's a herd of wild cattle nearby and I want to indicate which animal I think we should pursue. It's limping and hopefully will be the easiest one to catch. What do I do?

I point.

Revolutionary, right? I can see your eyes rolling from here.

Pointing is actually a big deal. Despite being closely related to us, chimps don't use pointing. Captive chimps can be trained to point, but it isn't something that comes easily. Yet well before a human baby can screech *"Doggie! Book! Candy!"* he or she is already using a pointed finger to, well, get the point across.[6]

Humans are extremely good at getting other humans to focus on something of mutual interest. We seem hardwired to communicate. After all, the environment selected us for our ability to live cooperatively. It selected us for our ability to share food *and* knowledge.

Let's get back to our hunt. Remember how I pointed at a limping cow? Now that I have focused your attention, I can communicate more information. Let's say you're a young, inexperienced hunter. I make a movement with my pointed finger to show which way I want you to go in order to cut off the cow's avenue of escape. I want to remind you to walk softly and slowly, so I mime the action. I huff to tell you to get going. The sharpness of my huff and an added hand-flutter tell you to hurry.

The better I am at communicating and teaching, and the better you are at understanding what I mean, the higher the likelihood we'll be

---

6   I applaud this baby's priorities.

feasting on cow tonight—and eating well in the future. Both of us will be more likely to survive and pass on our genes. However, for those who are bad teachers and poor learners . . . no cow for dinner. Probably no descendants, either.

It's likely teaching and language evolved in tandem. The soft tissue of the throat doesn't fossilize, so we aren't certain about Erectus's speech abilities, but small clues gleaned from Nariokotome Boy's skeleton suggest he didn't have the same kind of throat we do. He probably couldn't make the full range of sounds we make. Given his large Erectus brain, though, it's reasonable to assume that Nariokotome Boy could string together meaningful combinations of sounds and gestures. (More on language in Step 6.)

I hope by now it's obvious Erectus such as Nariokotome Boy were quite a bit like us. Erectus had our kind of body, and their brain size was getting closer to ours. Over many generations they had migrated over 14,000 kilometers (8,700 miles) across Asia, proving they were clever and adaptable. They knew a great deal about how to survive and could probably communicate well enough to share their knowledge through teaching.

What about their emotional lives? Did Erectus care about each other?

Empathy requires imagination. Unless you can see the world from someone else's point of view, you can't feel sympathy. We cringe when watching one of those skateboarder-wipe-out videos because we can conjure up the pain of hitting concrete.[7]

Theory of mind—as this ability is known—allows us to predict how others will think, feel, and act. We can use that ability for good or ill.

---

7   Okay, maybe some of you laugh instead. Humor, by the way, probably has deep evolutionary roots. Chimps laugh, which suggests that our common ancestor with chimps did, too. That means 7 million years of finding it funny when someone slips on a banana peel.

Humans aren't the only animals with theory of mind abilities. Ravens often hide food to save for later. If a raven notices another raven watching it hide food, it will switch the hiding place as soon as the spying raven's view is blocked—but not before. Chimps practice deception by waiting until a higher-ranking chimp is looking the other way before grabbing a hidden treat.

Male chimps, who are well-known for their aggressiveness, are also capable of remarkable empathy. Males sometimes adopt juveniles who have lost their mothers. The foster dad will share meat treats, let the orphan ride on his back, and defend the little one. You might expect a male to do this for a close relative that shares his genes. But these adoptions happen even when the foster father and the orphan aren't directly related.

Some 1.8-million-year-old Erectus fossils discovered in eastern Europe give us a clue about our ancestors' ability to feel for others. The group lived in a mixed habitat of grassland, woodland, and river canyons. It was a long-lost world of short-necked giraffes, giant ostriches, elephants, and rhinos. Once in a while the group probably scavenged a big carcass. But mostly they scratched out a living by hunting medium-sized animals like deer, antelopes, goats, sheep, and wild cattle. Their lives couldn't have been easy. They had to compete with (and watch out for) wolves, hyenas, giant cheetahs, and saber-toothed cats.

One skull found at the site belonged to an elderly man who had lost all but one of his teeth. Judging from the way his tooth sockets had been reabsorbed into his jawbone, the man had been almost entirely toothless for at least several years prior to his death. He was not in the kind of robust shape that would've allowed him to hunt or defend kills. How did he survive?

The skull of an elderly Erectus from Republic of Georgia (eastern Europe).

There's no way Grandpa could've chewed raw deer meat. Mashing meat with stone tools and eating softer things like berries and raw bone marrow would've helped. But the most likely scenario is that someone close to this man patiently chewed his food. Probably every day. Maybe every meal. They took food from their own mouth and gave it to him, bit by bit, to keep him alive.

Nowadays we have charities. It's a generous act to collect for UNICEF at Halloween, make cupcakes for a bake sale, or donate your extra clothes. Perhaps this 1.8-million-year-old act of kindness was the granddaddy of them all.

Using and controlling fire was a major advance for our ancestors

STEP 5
WE INVENT BARBECUE

Lightning stabs the savanna. For a moment everything is bleached by white light; the air crackles and shudders with thunder. Dark clouds sweep across the sky as the storm heads south.

The lightning has left a small spark behind. It catches on a stem of dry grass. Two stems, three stems. Now a clump. The spark becomes a ragged circle of flame. It eats its way through grass and scrub left parched by the dry season. Flying insects and birds take to the air, winging away from the smoke and flames. Panicked rats dart through the underbrush. In the distance the bigger animals—rhinos, elephants, lions, antelopes, buffaloes—catch the scent of disaster. Their ears swivel. They begin to move.

A group of hominins spot smoke rising against the horizon. They gather babies and toddlers and clutch stone tools. The band moves at a steady pace to keep ahead of the flames. After a few hours the brushfire hits a dry riverbed. Without fuel to burn, the flames die. Smoke drifts away on the wind.

Three elders turn back. The band follows. When they cross the riverbed, the elders spread out and walk in a line, their eyes scanning the blackened rubble. The rest of the band imitates the older ones. The elders remember the bounty a brushfire leaves behind: burnt rats, cooked snakes, baked tubers . . . and look! A charred gazelle. The hominins rush to the carcass. Their stone tools chop and cut and slash. They gather the pieces and set off toward a sheltered spot at the base of a rock outcrop.

One young hominin spies a piece of wood still glowing red. Driven by nothing but idle curiosity, he brings it along. While the others divvy up the bounty, our inquisitive young hominin lays half-burnt twigs across the glowing stick. A small fire flares to life. Fascinated, he offers it more. Disapproving hoots from the adults fail to discourage him. He feeds his fire as if it were a hungry pet. Other youngsters gather admiringly around the young fire-keeper. They offer the fire more fuel, squealing in excitement as it sparks and leaps.

One of the older hominins hands out chunks of gazelle meat. A few pieces have been well cooked by the wildfire, while other bits, sliced from deeper inside the carcass, are still raw. Our fire-keeper notices the cooked parts are tastier and easier to chew. Hmmm.

The boy tosses a piece of raw gazelle into the flames. The fire hisses and sizzles. When the meat cooks—or at least when it becomes less raw—he drags it out with a stick. The first bite burns his tongue. But the second bite is delicious.

He throws a few more sticks onto the fire. The adults huff in annoyance, but he ignores them. The other children eventually wander off, curl up, and fall asleep.

The young fire-keeper watches the fire as it dwindles into small lumps pulsing deep red. His brow furrows. *What if . . . ?*

Our youngster stands. He urinates into the fire, snickering in delight as the coals hiss and spit. When only sodden ash remains, he moves off to curl up against the warm back of an elder. The young hominin falls into a deep and contented sleep.

I'm guessing that story didn't end quite the way you expected. But here are a few things to consider.

First: I called our young fire-keeper a "hominin." I didn't specify Australopith, Handy Person, Erectus, or anything else. We don't really know which of our ancestors first used fire for cooking.

It's possible several different ancestors used fire in different places and at different times. But it's one thing to use fire now and then by chance. It's quite another thing to use fire regularly. It's yet another thing to pass fire-keeping and fire-making skills to others consistently, generation after generation. An innovation won't make much of an impact if it isn't shared. An innovation that isn't shared can't be improved upon by others, either. Think of those simple Oldowan tools. The technique of making sharp-edged stones was the basis for the improved Acheulean handaxe. Without the first, the second would never have happened.

A brushfire burns across the savanna.

The first use of fire by hominins probably involved lightning. Brush-fires triggered by lightning strikes are fairly common in the arid and semi-arid areas of Africa. Hominins living in these places would have been able to spot brushfire smoke from far away. Foraging in the rubble would have yielded the cooked bodies of animals that failed to escape—a great deal of food, potentially, for little effort. Digging would have exposed tubers baked by the fire as if in an underground oven.

Fire is incredibly useful. Cooking breaks down fibers, kills nasty parasites, and destroys many toxins. It widens the menu because it makes tough food easier to chew. And it makes sketchy foods like half-rotten carcasses and plants with chemical defenses safer to eat.

Remember how it takes lots of energy to run your brain? Next to your brain, your body's biggest energy guzzler is digestion. After you chew and swallow your food, it goes into your gut, where it is chemically taken apart and reassembled into forms your body can use. The digestion process burns energy. Cooked food, however, offers a shortcut. Cooked food requires less energy to chew and digest than uncooked food. If you can get by with a smaller gut, smaller teeth, and less powerful jaws, more of your body's energy is available for other things, like growing and powering a big brain.

Cooking offers other kinds of energy savings. Some foods are a lot easier to extract if they're cooked first. Many shellfish that are difficult to pry apart will pop open easily if heated. Tubers are much easier to peel and mash after cooking.

Fire can save energy in another way. When you're exposed to cold, your body burns energy to keep you warm. If you live in a cold climate, you can save calories by using a campfire to stay snug.

And where there's fire, there's smoke. If you're a naked and mostly hairless hominin who loves honey (the only real sugar rush available to our ancestors), you can avoid stings by smoking bees out of their hive. Smoke repels other biting insects, too. Fewer bites means you're less likely to suffer from insect-transmitted diseases. Smoke also preserves food. Longer-lasting food improves survival during lean times and allows hunters and gatherers to range more widely in search of food and shelter. And wooden tools like digging sticks can be hardened by smoking the wood over a fire.

That isn't the end of fire's advantages. In *The Jungle Book*, a scrawny young boy named Mowgli waves a flaming branch in Shere Khan's face, terrifying the murderous tiger into submission. The story is fictional, but not the basic idea. If you live in a world of lions, tigers, saber-tooths, leopards, wolves, and hyenas, fire provides protection. Especially at night when you are most vulnerable.

Once our ancestors mastered fire-starting, they could create their own brushfires at will. Dead animals could be collected later; live animals could be flushed toward hunters. Months later, as the burned area recovered, new grasses sprang up. The grazing animals attracted to the young, tender plants offered a second hunting opportunity.

Fire also extends the day. This would have been especially important to Erectus groups living farther north, where winter days are short. And, of course, a campfire brings people together. There's a practical aspect to this—cooking over one big fire is more efficient than making a bunch of little fires—but the campfire also offered social opportunities. As anyone who has ever attended middle school knows, in any group there will be cooperation, competition, and conflict. Even among friends.[1] The fireside was a place to form bonds and test bonds. A place to squabble and a place to work things out.

---

1   Maybe *especially* among friends.

So control of fire was a crucial step on the way to becoming human. But the exact origins of the technology aren't well understood.

Two East African sites from 1.6 million years ago offer the first evidence of fire use by hominins. Scientists think hominins were involved because campfires burn much hotter than natural fires and leave a different kind of mark on the surrounding rocks and soil. It's harder to tell exactly which hominin made the fire. Although Erectus was likely the first fire-user, we can't rule out Handy People. They were still around 1.6 million years ago, though they went extinct soon after.

There's other scattered evidence: burnt bones in Russia (eastern Europe) from 1.1 to 1 million years ago, burnt bones in South Africa at two sites from 1 million years ago and 700,000 years ago, and burnt wood and seeds in Israel (the Middle East) from 700,000 years ago. That's about it.

So when did hominins first begin to control fire on a regular basis? And how did this step impact human evolution?

The cooking hypothesis offers an intriguing explanation of how our evolution might be tied to the control of fire. According to this hypothesis, our ancestors (most likely Erectus) began controlling fire about 1.8 million years ago. Cooked food changed the direction of our evolution because if you eat a lot of cooked food, you don't need a big gut, powerful teeth, or powerful jaws.

Chimps and gorillas have flared rib cages to accommodate the big guts they need to process the plant material they eat. They also have bigger molars and heavier jaws to chomp up all those plants. But Erectus's rib cage was barrel shaped rather than flared; it had a small gut. Erectus also had smaller teeth and less powerful jaws than earlier hominins like Handy People or Australopiths. Even Erectus's bigger brain might be explained by the invention of cooking. The calories saved by cooking could have

A female Erectus cradles a flame.

allowed more energy to be directed toward brain growth.

I love the cooking hypothesis. It explains so much. The problem with it is this: there isn't a lot of data to back it up. If control of fire had been widespread enough to impact the evolution of our ancestors, we would expect to find more signs of it. But we have only the scattered evidence I mentioned earlier.

In science, data is everything. You can dream up the most elegant hypothesis ever, but if you don't have solid supporting data, your hypothesis won't be widely accepted by other scientists. The cooking hypothesis remains a "Well, *maybe*."

At this point you might be thinking: "Wait a minute. What about the theory of evolution itself? If evolution is 'just a theory,' why do these persnickety show-me-the-data scientists accept it? Why is it treated like a fact instead of a 'well, *maybe*' like the cooking hypothesis?"

So glad you asked.

In everyday conversation "I have a theory" means "I'm guessing." Maybe I have my reasons for thinking I know what will happen in the season finale of my favorite show, but I'm still guessing. In science, though, "theory" has a more formal meaning. A theory is a well-tested, widely accepted explanation for a whole constellation of facts, observations, and data. The overwhelming data in support of evolution comes from fossils, observations of living populations, laboratory experiments, and genetics. The evidence in support of the theory of evolution through natural selection is as solid as the evidence supporting Newton's and Einstein's theories about gravity.

And now back to the cooking hypothesis.

Other scientists have pointed out that cooking isn't necessary to explain the hominin trend toward small guts, smaller teeth, less powerful jaws, and bigger brains. Mashing food with tools and eating lots of the softer bits of prey (guts, marrow, and brains) would also allow for less chewing and easier digestion while providing the high-quality nutrition needed for a big brain.

Even if fire isn't responsible for our small guts, small teeth, weak jaws, and big brains, as the cooking hypothesis claims, it seems to have

Striking flints to make a fire.

impacted our evolution another way. All modern humans have a mutated gene that makes wood smoke less toxic to us than to other primates. The sitting-around-campfires environment of our ancestors—an environment they themselves created—selected individuals with this protective muta- tion. Because the individuals with the mutation out-reproduced the ones who weren't so lucky, the mutation spread far and wide. It's now part of our genetic inheritance.[2]

It did seem to take a long time for fire to become a regular part of our ancestors' lives. The scattered evidence of fire control between 1.6 million and 700,000 years ago suggests fire-keeping happened in different areas and at different times but didn't stick. There was a spark now and then, but it didn't spread. It dwindled and died like a fire that isn't tended.

---

2   Don't use this as an excuse to pick up any bad habits. Smoke is LESS toxic for us, not NON-toxic.

Even the most important innovations aren't always greeted with enthusiasm. Not so long ago, people asked: "Why would I want a mobile phone?"[3]

The benefits of fire seem obvious to us. Not so, perhaps, to hominins who already had their own ways of preparing food or scaring off predators. Fire is a difficult technology to master. If you haven't yet figured out how to start a fire using friction, then you need to keep your fire going 24/7 so it doesn't go out. That would take effort and cooperation. There would always be the danger of the fire being extinguished by wind or rain or inattention. And you'd need to figure out how to carry the fire with you whenever your band moved.

But let's say a few groups of Erectus realized the advantages of a good campfire. And let's imagine that some of them noticed sparks flying when certain types of rocks (pyrites and flint) were struck together during toolmaking. Perhaps someone spotted smoke rising when they drilled a hole in a piece of wood by twirling a stick rapidly between their palms. Even if one band of Erectus, or two, or three, figured out how to control fire, that didn't necessarily mean the technology would spread.

Many factors influence whether or not an innovation sticks. The most basic is population size. If there are very few users of the innovation, crucial knowledge may be lost because of some random event. If the only Erectus band that controlled fire got wiped out by disease, or a volcanic eruption, their knowledge would die with them.

Or perhaps the fire-savvy hominins lived in an isolated valley. Their innovation might never travel over the surrounding mountain ridges. Or maybe they shared their knowledge with neighbors, but those neighbors were too thickheaded to understand the advantages. And then there's the problem of transferring knowledge to the next generation. Fire-starting in

---

3　These are the same kind of people who still can't figure out how to download an app.

particular involves lots of detailed information. If the members of the fire-keeping band were poor teachers and their offspring were poor learners, there wouldn't be much hope of keeping the technology alive long enough for it to spread to other groups.

Luckily some of our ancestors saw the light. We can imagine it happening here and there, in fits and starts, at the cost of much frustration and many burnt fingers. The first hominin that we know used fire consistently was a new species: *Homo heidelbergensis*. Heidelbergensis is our "parent" species, so to speak. Scientists think we are probably their direct descendants.

Once again, credit our African homeland for a demanding environment that selected the brainiest individuals. You wouldn't have noticed from generation to generation, of course. Every individual would've looked as similar to their parents as you do to yours. But small differences added up. By 700,000 years ago, an Erectus population in Africa had evolved into Heidelbergensis. Based on the size of their skulls, Heidelbergensis had a larger brain than Erectus (1,200 cc compared to Erectus's 1,000 cc). And yes—at last!—at this point our ancestors were definitely brainier than dolphins.

The Erectus population in Africa died out after Heidelbergensis evolved. However, a few Erectus populations survived in Asia. By the time Heidelbergensis showed up (by 700,000 years ago), all the Australopiths and Handy People were long gone. Only their fossils and stone tools remained, buried under layers of ash and dirt, waiting to be excavated by modern scientists.

Heidelbergensis, the newest member of the *Homo* family, spread across Africa, the Middle East, Asia, and into Europe, traveling as far north as England. (At that time sea levels were so low you could walk from mainland Europe to Great Britain.) Control of fire made it possible for Heidelbergensis to survive in Europe's game-rich but cold environments.

A large cleaver made by a Heidelbergensis sometime between 800,000 and 300,000 years ago in Mauritania (West Africa) was shaped around two round marks that give it a distinct face. Cat? Crocodile? Was this object passed around a campfire, discussed, and admired?

By 400,000 years ago Heidelbergensis used fire pits regularly. From so simple a beginning many other advances would someday flow: container cooking, fired pottery, metalworking, and s'mores.

Let's imagine a band of Heidelbergensis living in Germany about 400,000 years ago. This isn't the Germany of cuckoo clocks and juicy sausages. This is the Germany of mammoths, elephants, woolly rhinos, wild horses, wild cattle, bison, cave lions, giant hyenas, and cave bears.

It's evening. Our Heidelbergensis group relaxes around their campfire, knowing the flames will discourage night-hunting predators. The Heidelbergensis are more sturdily built than modern humans. Their sloping foreheads and thick brow ridges give them a stereotypical—I hate to say it—"caveman" look. But you would definitely recognize the way they cluster companionably around their hearth.

It's getting late; the last bits of horse meat have been shared and the last smudges of fat licked off fingers. A few rodents-on-a-stick are propped over the coals for tomorrow's breakfast. Adults cradle sleepy little ones in their arms. The older children pile together like puppies.

We're probably close enough to these Heidelbergensis to guess what they would do as the campfire glows and the shadows dance all around. It's the same thing we would do.

They would talk.

A male Homo heidelbergensis.

STEP 6
WE START TALKING (AND NEVER SHUT UP)

When we humans are good at something, we're *really* good at it. New Caledonian crows construct stick tools; we construct suspension bridges. Meerkats teach their young how to handle a scorpion; we teach our children how to handle algebra. African wild dogs cooperate to bring down an antelope; we cooperate to send satellites into orbit.

It's the same with language. In the wild, chimps, bonobos, and gorillas use simple gestures and sounds. When captive great apes are taught sign language, most can put together (at best) simple two- or three-word statements using a vocabulary of 200 to 300 words.

Human toddlers spontaneously use many of the same gestures as wild chimps, bonobos, and gorillas. Yet by the time a toddler becomes a high schooler, he or she knows about 60,000 words. A well-read adult may be familiar with 150,000.

We humans can communicate anything we can think of. We do this by combining a large vocabulary of words with a set of rules (grammar). Grammar allows us to manipulate words to produce an infinite variety of meanings. It allows us to be very specific about when, where, why, how, and to whom something is happening . . . has happened . . . or will happen. And let's not forget that human language is much more than speech. It can also be expressed through gestures (sign language) or symbols (writing).

Our extraordinary language abilities must have evolved for a reason. What advantages did language offer our ancestors? How did it aid their survival and reproduction?

ADVANTAGE #1: TEACHING AND LEARNING

If you're trying to pass crucial skills to your offspring, language makes teaching and learning quicker and easier. Language is particularly useful when communicating a complex, multi-step skill like fire-starting.

ADVANTAGE #2: PLANNING AND COOPERATION

Language enhances cooperation. Cooperative food-gatherers can use language to plan a hunt or a foraging trip, and they can share those plans with others. Planning itself is a very brainy ability because it requires the ability to time travel. Time travel isn't science fiction. It's something we do all the time, inside our own heads, whenever we think about the past or the future.

ADVANTAGE #3: SCHMOOZING

Language enhances our social life. We are group-living animals who need the cooperation of others to survive. Any ability that can help us socially is likely to be selected by our social environment. Just think of language as a super-fancy substitute for lice and tick removal.

Yes, you heard me correctly.

Apes spend a lot of time plucking parasites out of each other's fur. When one chimp, bonobo, or gorilla grooms another, it's their way of saying: "I like you, and I want you to like me." Scientists think humans may use language as a kind of "verbal grooming." We stroke those we are closest to with words.[1]

---

1   Though given the state of personal hygiene 600,000 years ago, we probably also appreciated a friendly lice-picking session.

A group of bonobos grooming each other.

Want to know which bonobos are most closely bonded? Measure the time they spend picking lice and ticks off each other. Want to know which humans are most closely bonded? Measure how much free time they spend talking (or texting or emailing or using sign language) with each other. Bonobos, however, can de-louse only one friend at a time. Using language, we can schmooze with an entire buddy group all at once.

Heidelbergensis were likely the first hominins possessing something resembling modern human language. We know they had the necessary processing power because their brains were almost as big as ours. And the existence of those Acheulean handaxes tells us their brains were already "wired," so to speak, for fine muscle control.

If you're wondering what fine muscle control has to do with language, say "see" followed by "key." The difference is a tiny tongue adjustment.

Around 500,000 years ago, in Kathu Pan, South Africa, a Heidelbergensis shaped a piece of ironstone into a handaxe of extraordinary beauty and symmetry.

Other great apes don't have that kind of precise control.[2] Luckily, thanks to the long toolmaking heritage of Australopiths, Handy People, Erectus, and Heidelbergensis, our ancestors had already evolved the brain circuits necessary for nimble fingers, a good handgrip, and excellent hand-eye coordination. A similar kind of precise coordination between lips, tongue, and throat is required for sophisticated language.

Evolution's a real couch potato. It settles for whatever's within reach. If pre-existing brain wiring works for toolmaking, might as well use it for sound-making. Remember evolution's stirring motto? *Yeah. Good enough.*

Heidelbergensis's big brain required time to develop. As you might recall, Erectus children developed twice as fast as modern humans, so at eight or nine years old, Nariokotome Boy was already an adolescent. But by the time of Heidelbergensis, growth rates were slowing down and becoming more human-like.

From the standpoint of evolution, it's risky to grow up slowly. You might starve, die of disease, get gored by a bison, or fall off a cliff before you get a chance to reproduce. On the other hand, if your survival is based upon growing a big brain and cramming it full of environmental knowledge, social skills, language, and technology, that brain is going to need time to reach its full potential. An intelligent animal needs to play. To practice. The survival advantages of our slow-developing brains were apparently worth the risks.

That bigger Heidelbergensis brain also changed childbirth. A newborn chimp's head is small enough to fit easily through its mother's pelvis. The baby slips out, and Mom scoops up her little one. No big fuss. Australopiths, who had a brain-to-body ratio similar to chimps, would likely have had relatively easy births. Handy People had bigger brains and

---

2 Although great apes do have some vocal control. To prove this, scientists taught captive orangutans to play the kazoo. Seriously . . . an ape kazoo orchestra. *Please* let them go on tour!

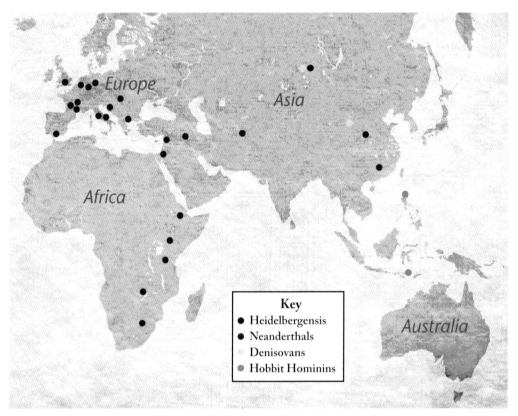

Major sites where fossils of Homo heidelbergensis *(Heidelbergensis),* Homo neanderthalensis *(Neanderthals),* Denisovans, Homo floresiensis *(Flores Hobbits), and* Homo luzonensis *(Luzon Hobbits) have been found. Modern coastlines are shown for clarity.*

probably a bit more difficulty. Erectus births were getting uncomfortable.

By the time of Heidelbergensis, the hominin brain had enlarged to the point that an infant's head could just barely fit through its mother's pelvis. It's the same today. You know how in movies women are always moaning in pain during childbirth? They're not wimps. Human births are unusually difficult—more difficult than the births of any other mammal. Since female hips can't get any wider without sacrificing efficient upright walking, generations of natural selection have produced a few helpful adaptations. In humans (and likely in Heidelbergensis as well), the joints of pregnant women soften and spread prior to labor. This offers the baby's head a smidgen more space. A baby's body also does a half turn during normal childbirth so the head fits the shape of the gap better. And a newborn's skull is composed of soft plates designed to compress and even overlap as the baby squeezes through. Only later does the skull harden.

Despite these evolutionary adjustments for its monster head, a human infant must still be born underbaked (so to speak). Its brain is far less developed at birth than those of other mammals. A human is eighteen months old before he or she can move around and cling to Mom as well as a newborn chimp. Exiting the womb early in its development allows a human baby to have the largest possible brain *before* birth while still having the opportunity to develop *after* birth.

Infant helplessness comes at a cost. A human baby needs a lot of care for a long period of time. This intensive support is possible only among a group-living, highly social, highly cooperative species. It truly takes a village (or in this case, a clan of hominins) to raise a child.

Sometime after 500,000 years ago, as those sturdy, fire-making Heidelbergensis spread across Africa, Europe, and into Asia, the different environments they lived in selected different traits. The Heidelbergensis population in Europe evolved into *Homo neanderthalensis* (the Neanderthals). The Neanderthals later spread into the Middle East. Eventually some of them reached Siberia (northern Asia). The Asian Heidelbergensis population evolved into another hominin: the Denisovans. The African Heidelbergensis population evolved into us—*Homo sapiens*. (You'll read more about us in Step 7.) Heidelbergensis is our "parent" species, so to speak. Neanderthals and Denisovans are our "sibling" species.

Only a few Denisovan bones have been uncovered. The species is largely a mystery. But most of us have heard of the Neanderthals, named after the valley in Germany where their remains were first discovered.

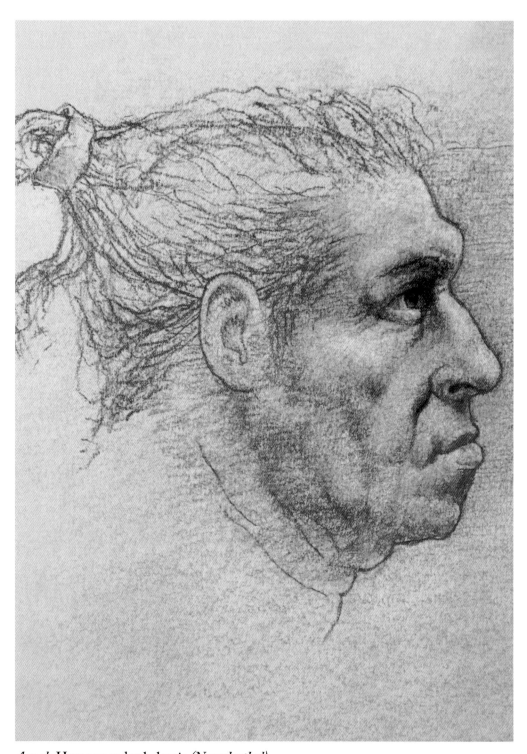

A male Homo neanderthalensis *(Neanderthal).*

Neanderthals have gotten a bad rap. For years they were depicted as knuckle-dragging cavemen with the IQ of a potato. The reality is quite different. In Neanderthals we glimpse the beginnings of everything we consider distinctively human. Neanderthals were us—except tougher.

The environment tests and the environment selects. The environment in Europe selected qualities that aided survival in a cold climate. The bodies of Neanderthals were even stockier than those of Heidelbergensis because a thick build helps retain heat. Neanderthals probably had lighter skin, which makes it easier to absorb vitamin D from the meager sunlight farther north. Their larger, fleshier noses warmed up frigid air before it was sucked down into their lungs. Neanderthals were also heavily muscled. If you make a living shoving spears into woolly rhinos at close range, you'd better have some serious strength and coordination. Neanderthals would crush it at the Olympics.

Neanderthals had both brains and brawn. You might assume modern human brains are the biggest hominin brains of all time. Nope. Our brains average 1,350 cc. Both pre-modern humans (before 10,000 years ago) and Neanderthals had brains averaging over 1,400 cc.[3]

Did Neanderthals have the same language skills we do? Well, maybe they didn't have the past perfect participle pancreatic verb form,[4] but it's likely Neanderthals had some level of speech. Which brings us to FOXP2.

FOXP2 is not a new video game. It's a gene connected to language ability. Scientists don't fully understand FOXP2's function, but people born with a defective FOXP2 gene have trouble putting sentences together. It's as if their language app didn't fully download. Chimps have a FOXP2 gene, too, but the chimp version is different from the human version. Somewhere down the line—perhaps by the time of

---

3   Ouch.

4   Actually, we don't, either. I made that up.

Heidelbergensis—our original chimp-like FOXP2 acquired two crucial mutations that help our brains process language.

If you recall, a mutation happens when genes are reshuffled and recopied during reproduction. A mutation is a copying mistake. Most genetic mutations make no difference at all, but every once in a while a mutation makes a difference. If that mutation hurts the organism's survival chances, the organism will probably die early and the harmful mutation won't be passed on. If an organism has a helpful mutation, though, that organism is more likely to survive and reproduce. The more helpful the mutation, the faster the mutation will spread through the population.

Based on a genetic analysis of DNA from their bones, we know Neanderthals had the same FOXP2 gene we do. Neanderthals also had a hyoid bone similar to ours. The hyoid is a slender, curved bone in our throat that connects to ligaments and muscles. The presence of a human-like hyoid bone suggests some degree of human-like control over sounds.

Complex human language also demands a special kind of ear. After all, what does it matter if you can make subtly varied sounds like "see" and "key" if the other person can't hear the difference? Studies of their tiny fossilized ear bones suggest Neanderthals could hear sounds in the same range as modern human speech.

How far back do these language-related traits go? If two closely related species share a trait, it's likely that the trait was inherited from their common ancestor. If Neanderthals and humans have the same FOXP2 gene, similar hyoid bones, and similar ear bones, we probably inherited those traits—or a version of those traits—from Heidelbergensis.

Which means our other "sibling" species, the Denisovans, probably inherited adaptations for language, too. But we won't know for sure until scientists uncover more Denisovan fossils.

Let's imagine the lives of Neanderthals living in Europe hundreds of thousands of years ago. If they could speak (even if not as skillfully as we do), what did they yak-yak-yak about?

Most likely other people.

Evolution predisposes us to crave salt, sugar, and fat because we couldn't always get enough of these important nutrients in our ancestral environments.[5] Evolution also predisposes us to crave gossip. If survival depends on being part of a tight-knit group, what you think of others and what they think of you *matters*. Who's a friend and who's a rival? Who's mating with whom, and how does that affect your chances of reproducing? Do your group-mates respect you? Who's trustworthy and who's a cheater? And oh, by the way . . . are there any murderous maniacs around?

A 400,000-year-old early Neanderthal from Spain was discovered with two identically shaped gouges in the front of his skull. The man had been *twice* bashed in the forehead by the same sharp object. You don't have to be Sherlock Holmes to deduce this wasn't an accident. Maybe two people got into an argument; maybe two groups fought over territory. Whatever the details, this is the oldest evidence of someone ending up dead by someone else's hand. If there were witnesses, and words to describe it, I guarantee this was talked about. *A lot.*

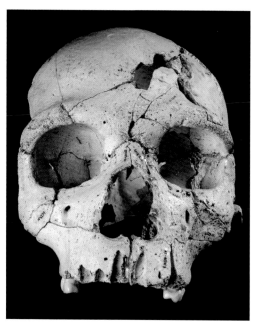

This 400,000-year-old skull shows the marks of having been struck twice in the forehead by the same object.

---

5   Excuse me while I forage for salted caramel ice cream.

Food, and how to get it, was probably another main topic of conversation. *Who's going berry-picking today, and who's going hunting? Which prey animal should we target? Once we've killed the deer, who gets what?* Deciding how to divide up the goodies requires negotiation.[6]

Maybe some Neanderthals talked about the latest in high-tech weaponry: the spear. The oldest ever discovered are 300,000-year-old wooden shafts with sharpened tips from a Neanderthal site in Germany. Scientists discovered the spears near the remains of ten butchered horses.

Spears might not seem like a big deal. But a weapon that allowed us to kill from distance, even a short distance, gave us a better chance against desperate prey fighting with teeth, claws, hooves, antlers, or horns. We could now bring down large animals in the prime of life. Spears made us—at long last—the equals of lions.

We have no idea what words Neanderthals used to describe spears, lions, hunting, or anything else. We do know that in every human culture, standards emerge for how to do things. We can imagine that our ancestors developed standards for how to communicate and over time those standards became more elaborate. This sound means "spear." This combination of sounds (or sounds and gestures) means "to thrust a spear."

As language became increasingly sophisticated, it helped us transfer complex skills from generation to generation. Those 300,000-year-old spears from Germany might look simple, but they were carefully designed. The spears were carved so the tips came from the hardest part of the tree (near the base of the trunk). Each spear's center of gravity is about a third of the distance from the tip—the same balance as modern Olympic javelins.

Better communication between teacher and learner will produce a better spear. A better spear means more food for you and your offspring.

---

6   As opposed to bashing someone in the head. Use your words, Neanderthals!

Spears made by Neanderthals in Germany (western Europe) 300,000 years ago. Each is about 2 meters (6.5 feet) long.

There's also evidence Neanderthals made composite tools (a shaft, a stone blade, and a binding). Consider this: putting together a multipart tool is like arranging words into a sentence. A stone tip is useful; so is a binding material and a wooden shaft. But when assembled in the right sequence, these things become something greater than the sum of their parts. In a similar way, individual words can be assembled into the sentence "We kill horses with spears."

Neanderthals possessed many other complex skills. They prepared hides with bone tools, fashioned clothing, cooked plants, and twisted fibers to make cords. They were adept at hunting woodland game but versatile enough to exploit seafood. Neanderthals in coastal areas ate crabs, eels, seabirds, clams, and mussels—all of which require different hunting and gathering techniques. Fossil evidence suggests some Neanderthals had "swimmer's ear," a condition common among people who spend a lot of time in the water. Were these Neanderthals shallow-water divers?

The Neanderthal eye for beauty: a 300,000-year-old handaxe from England (western Europe) was fashioned to frame a fossilized shell embedded in the stone.

Unfortunately, Neanderthal conversations are lost to us. We don't know how they experienced the world or what they thought about it. We do have some hints about their relationships with each other. Remember that old, toothless Erectus who probably needed help to survive? There's evidence at least some Neanderthals took care of the aged and disabled. The remains of one elderly man show he had a withered arm, a deformed leg and foot, and an old facial injury that probably left him blind in one eye. He could not have survived without the help of his group-mates.

And a Neanderthal child born with a severe birth defect was cared for and survived until she was about ten.

Hints about Neanderthal child-rearing come to us through a collection of 80,000-year-old Neanderthal footprints discovered on a French beach. (The sand later hardened into stone.) The prints belonged to a group of ten to fourteen people, mostly children and adolescents. Based on footprint size, the youngest was about two. One set of prints probably belonged to a large male. Was this Neanderthal day care?

On the flip side, there's also evidence of Neanderthal cannibalism. Neanderthal bones with cut marks have been found at Neanderthal hearths. The cannibalism might have been of the Donner Party variety: while stuck in the snow, starving and desperate, a group of Neanderthals ate the bodies of those who had already succumbed. It's also possible some Neanderthals deliberately hunted other Neanderthals. They may have seen their "in-group" as deserving of kindness and some "out-groups" as deserving of cruelty. If so, it's a trait shared by modern humans.

Perhaps eating the bodies of the dead was part of a funeral ritual. Which raises the question: Did Neanderthals have a spiritual life? Maybe a Neanderthal could say: "Make spear like this!" or "Come here!" But did a Neanderthal wonder: "After me die, what happen?"

Neanderthals sometimes buried their dead. Perhaps this was purely practical: if you bury a decomposing corpse, it's less likely to attract predators. But if you're digging a grave only to discourage hyenas, there's no reason to carefully position the body, as scientists have discovered at several Neanderthal sites.

Here's something else to puzzle over. About 176,500 years ago, a group of Neanderthals ventured far—very far—into a cave in France. They went 336 meters (367 yards) into the pitch-black interior and would've needed torches to light their way. What were the Neanderthals searching for in that inky darkness? Why did they break stalagmites off the cave's floor and arrange them into two large circles, one smaller one, and four separate piles? It's as if they were creating their own sunless Stonehenge.

Yes, something was definitely going on inside those big Neanderthal brains. Yet no matter how much insight and intelligence they possessed, they could not have imagined what was coming. The Neanderthals were about to cross paths with some lanky, dark-skinned, egg-headed immigrants from the south.

Us.

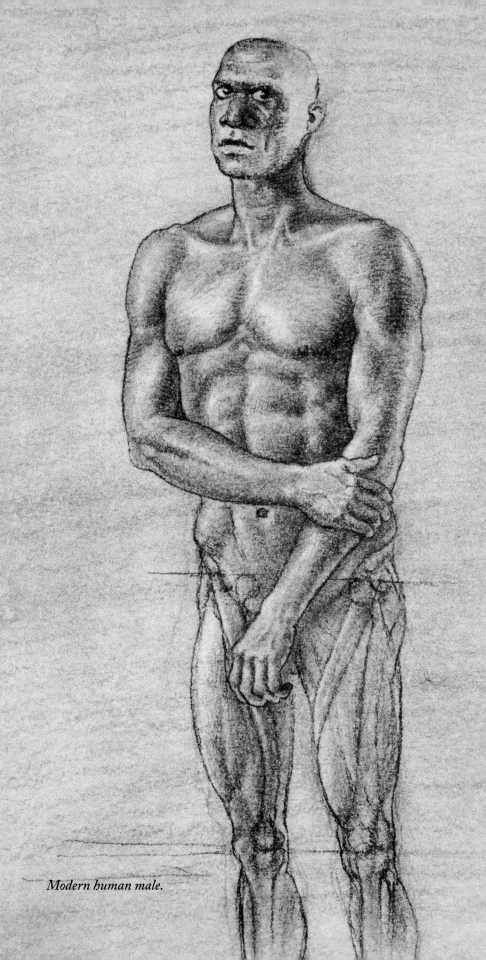

Modern human male.

STEP 7
WE BECOME STORYTELLERS

You might be wondering: "What's the difference between Step 6 (We Start Talking) and Step 7 (We Become Storytellers)? If you can talk, you can tell a story, right?"

Yes, language is part of storytelling. But being able to string together subject, verb, and object ("I found berries") is not exactly *The Lord of the Rings*. Storytelling is language on steroids. And spoken language is only one way of telling a story.

Becoming storytellers is about reaching a fully modern capacity for communicating and understanding complex stories. Stories about what happened once upon a time, stories about what's happening right now, stories about what might happen in the future, and stories about what could happen only in our imagination. I'm talking about the point in our evolution when—if we could magically go back in time and tell the story in their language—our ancestors would understand *Star Wars*.

Of course we'd have to make adjustments. The Stormtroopers would need to ditch their blaster rifles and fling spears instead.[1] But the dramatic chases, the friends who cooperate and compete, the serious father-son conflict? Our ancestors would recognize it all. It would attract their

---

1   And they would still miss.

attention just as it attracts ours. At that point in our evolution, they are us and we are them.

But let's rewind to the hazy dawn of our species: *Homo sapiens.*

Once again, it started in Africa. Maybe in the rift valleys; maybe in several parts of the continent. Once again, we can probably thank a wildly erratic climate for selecting the sharpest knives in the drawer. "Sharp knife" is appropriate because a new tool kit made its first appearance about 320,000 years ago in Kenya (East Africa). Compared to those hefty Acheulean handaxes our ancestors clutched for a solid million years, these blades were smaller, finer, and sharper. Their manufacture required even greater skill. The people who made these new blades also ground powder from ochre (a mineral). Ochre has practical uses: as an insect repellent, preservative, and glue ingredient. But it also comes in a range of earthy colors from yellow to red to black. Mix ground ochre with animal fat and you've got paint. Maybe these people were using ochre to make art.

We're not sure who made these new blades and ground ochre. A late version of Heidelbergensis? Or an early version of *Homo sapiens?*

The oldest fossil that might be *Homo sapiens* is a 300,000-year-old skull discovered in Morocco (North Africa). It has a flat face and thin brow ridges like a modern human. Yet the skull shape (long rather than rounded like ours) and the large teeth are closer to those of Heidelbergensis. Perhaps this is evolution caught in midstride. Tools found at the site are like the ones from East Africa—light, sharp, and skillfully worked.

A 259,000-year-old partial skull discovered in South Africa may also represent an early member of our species. Other fossils found in Ethiopia (East Africa) dated as early as 190,000 years ago have our teeth, our skull shape, and our slender frame. They are the first physically modern humans. Some of these early humans left Africa, leaving 210,000-year-old bones in

300,000-year-old stone tools found in Morocco (West Africa).

Greece (southern Europe) and 180,000-year-old bones in Israel (the Middle East). These early adventurers appear to have died out, though there's now evidence some of them were absorbed into local Neanderthal populations.

Even though we know humans living around 200,000 years ago *looked* like us, we don't know if they *thought* like us. We can't do our time-traveling road show of *Star Wars* to see if they gasp when Darth Vader says to Luke: "I am your father!"[2] We must rely on other evidence.

To explore whether our ancestors thought like us, scientists ask: Did they have language as complex as ours? More importantly, did they use complex symbols? These two qualities distinguish human minds from all

---

2   Oops. Belated spoiler alert.

others. And it's no exaggeration to call these abilities superpowers.[3]

SUPERPOWER #1: SPEAKING A COMPLEX LANGUAGE

Take two human babies from two different places on Earth, swap them, and each will grow up speaking the language of their adopted parents with perfect fluency. Even if that language has tones (like Vietnamese) or tones *and* clicks (like !Xóõ from South Africa).

Complex language is a human universal. That suggests it evolved in our ancestors *before* they left Africa. If fully modern language evolved *after* we spread around the globe, we would expect some populations (the ones that developed complex language first) to have better language abilities than others. But that's not the case. Most children learn language with ridiculous ease. And though you might assume complex societies produce the most complex languages, that's not so. Tuyuca, a language spoken by less than a thousand people in the Amazon rain forest, may be the world's most difficult. (Though it's a breeze to learn if you're raised Tuyucan.)

SUPERPOWER #2: COMMUNICATING WITH SYMBOLS

A symbol is something used to represent something else. Language is a kind of symbolism because you're using a sound (or in sign language, a gesture) to represent an object or idea. However, language is just one form of symbolic communication.

If I say the word "lion," it's a puff of air coming out of my mouth. If I paint a picture of a lion, it's a collection of chemicals smeared on paper. If I carve a little lion from a piece of wood, it's a whittled bit of dead tree. If I write the word "lion," it's a combination of straight and curved lines.

---

3   No adamantium, super-soldier serum, gamma rays, radioactive spider bites, or intervention by Greek gods required.

None of these things is an actual lion. None comes *close* to being a dangerous predator that can break a zebra's neck. Yet each of these symbols sends a "lion" thought from my brain to yours.

I'm sure zebras have thoughts about lions, too. Usually last thoughts. But not symbolic ones.

Captive chimps and bonobos have been taught to communicate with their trainers through sign language or by pointing to symbols on a board. This suggests that a capacity for symbolic thinking is part of our great ape heritage. There's evidence of symbolic thought among early hominins, too. Remember the 500,000-year-old mussel shell engraved with a zigzag pattern by Erectus? And the far older Makapansgat Pebble, collected by an Australopith? The Makapansgat Pebble is a symbol powerful enough to communicate "face" across time, space, and species.

It's clear modern humans have complex language and symbolic communication. You're reading this book, after all. Figuring out when our ancestors evolved these superpowers is trickier. After all, they didn't have writing. We'll never hear the tales they told around their campfires. Their music and songs faded millennia ago, and their lifeless bones can't leap up to perform their dances. We must rely on physical objects like engravings, paintings, sculpture, and jewelry to figure out what went on inside those long-dead brains.

You might be surprised to find jewelry on this list. But personal adornment tells a story. Jewelry, tattoos, piercings, hairstyle, clothing, and makeup (the modern version of body paint) are all symbols meant to be read by others. They communicate who we are.

Shell beads pop up as early as 135,000 years ago in Algeria (North Africa) and Israel (the Middle East). One hundred thousand years ago,

A chunk of engraved ochre with a design carved 77,000 years ago.

humans in South Africa used an abalone shell as a paint-pot for liquefied ochre. Were they painting on rock walls? Or using their own skin as a canvas? And the ochre itself was sometimes decorated; a 77,000-year-old chunk found at the same site has engraved crosshatch patterns.[4]

So far we've focused on our direct ancestors. But let's not forget our sibling species. Remember those rings of broken stalagmites assembled by Neanderthals deep inside a cave? Those rings appear symbolic, even if we don't understand the symbolism. About 130,000 years ago Neanderthals in Croatia (eastern Europe) made necklaces from eagle talons. Around 115,000 years ago Neanderthals in Spain (western Europe) drilled holes in seashells and painted them with red and yellow pigments. Somebody was dressed to impress.

For a long time we *Homo sapiens* considered ourselves the first hominins to make paintings. That might not be correct. As far back as 64,000 years ago, someone entered a cave in Spain and painted dots, squares,

4   #WorldsFirstHashtag.

and lines on the walls. Since the first *Homo sapiens* didn't reach Europe until 18,000 years later, the graffiti artists were most likely Neanderthals.

Meanwhile, back in Africa . . .

Given our intellectual superpowers, you might think that we *Homo sapiens* walked a straight line to world domination. A rapid migration to the four corners of the planet, quickly followed by the invention of agriculture, cities, the printing press, and the Marvel Comics Universe.

Not so fast. About 150,000 years ago, we almost went the way of the dodo.

The evidence of our near-extinction is in our DNA. Humans have low genetic diversity, which suggests that at one point, at least, human numbers were low. This population dip might have been caused by a climate crisis. Past climate swings likely spurred the evolution of our intelligence and adaptability, but between 400,000 and 100,000 years ago,

Ochre figures painted on the wall of a cave in Spain (western Europe).

climate instability caused repeated wet/dry cycles severe enough to turn us into an endangered species. Like modern pandas, minus the cuteness.

The environment wasn't out to get us. It wasn't out to save us, either. Our fate was in our hands.

The struggling remnants of humanity may have taken refuge along the coast of South Africa and survived off the year-round supply of shell-fish. Or perhaps they retreated to the shrinking wetlands of south-central Africa. But around 120,000 years ago, the cold and dry conditions eased. Our population increased.

Sometime before 100,000 years ago, a second wave of migrants left Africa and moved into the Middle East. At the time the Middle East was a landscape of woodlands and grasslands like East Africa. It was home to many of the same species—antelope, ostrich, lions, hyenas, and hippos. But when our ancestors arrived, they met something they didn't expect: the Neanderthals.

Today we're the only surviving hominin. But when we left Africa, our world was like Tolkien's Middle-earth with its Orcs, Ents, Elves, Dwarves, Hobbits, and humans.[5] Neanderthals lived in the Middle East and Europe. In Central Asia they overlapped with the Denisovans. In addition there were two kinds of Hobbit-like hominins living on islands in Southeast Asia. (More about them later.)

As you may recall, Denisovans were one of three species that evolved from different populations of Heidelbergensis. We humans evolved from African Heidelbergensis, Neanderthals evolved from European Heidelbergensis, and Denisovans evolved from Asian Heidelbergensis.

As everyone knows, families are complicated.

---

5   A more complete list would of course include the Valar, the Istari, Beornings, Balrogs, river spirits, giants, trolls, and Tom Bombadil. Not that I would ever get nerdy on you.

A 50,000-year-old Homo neanderthalensis *skull (left) and a 100,000-year-old* Homo sapiens *skull (right), both found in Israel (the Middle East).*

Denisovans looked much like Neanderthals, though their fingers were slender (more like human hands) and their heads wider. And based on clues in their DNA, Denisovans may have interbred with another hominin— possibly Erectus. Incredibly, Erectus survived on the island of Java in Southeast Asia until about 110,000 years ago. We probably just missed meeting them.

Our interactions with Neanderthals must've been interesting. We had similar brain sizes and (presumably) similar mental lives. We had similar technologies (fire, stone tools). Having evolved under the African sun, we were dark skinned. Analysis of the Neanderthal genome tells us some Neanderthals had red hair and light-brown skin. Neanderthals were shorter but sturdier and stronger, while we were taller and skinnier. In a hand-to-hand fight, you'd bet on the Neanderthal. But hey, we could outrun them.

We do know one really interesting detail about what some Neanderthals and humans did when they met. They mated. Scientists discovered this by comparing genetic material from modern human blood samples to genetic material extracted from Neanderthal bones. The genome of all modern descendants of the first successful human migration out of Africa—which means every living person with ancestors from Europe, Asia, the Americas, or Oceania—is 1 to 2 percent Neanderthal. People with all-African ancestry also have some Neanderthal genes. Scientists think that around 20,000 years ago, some early Europeans with Neanderthal genes migrated back into Africa and mixed with those who hadn't migrated.

There's a little bit of Neanderthal in every cell in my body. Yours, too.

Human/Neanderthal mixing wasn't limited to a single period or a single place. As you may recall, the first adventurous humans to leave Africa didn't survive as a separate population. But they did leave behind some descendants—Neanderthals who carried human DNA. Later, in Europe, Neanderthals and humans would overlap for thousands of years. A genetic analysis of human bones around 40,000 years old from eastern Europe revealed a man with a Neanderthal ancestor just four generations back.

We don't know if sexual violence was involved in these couplings. We also can't discount star-crossed, cross-species love. By comparing the genomes of mouth bacteria found in Neanderthals (taken from plaque on fossil teeth) and modern humans, scientists discovered that both kinds descended from a common bacterium shared by Neanderthals and humans about 100,000 years ago.

Hmm. How would Neanderthals and humans swap mouth bacteria?

Neanderthals and humans weren't the only crossbreeding hominins.

DNA from a tiny finger bone (brown object atop the pinkie finger) was used to identify Denisovans as a new hominin species.

As Neanderthals expanded eastward, they met Denisovans. In Denisova Cave in Siberia (Asia), researchers discovered 90,000-year-old bone scraps belonging to a girl, nicknamed "Denny," who had a Neanderthal mother and a Denisovan father. Denny was a first-generation hominin hybrid.

When we humans reached mainland Asia by at least 80,000 years ago, we also interbred with Denisovans. As a result, people all over Asia are a little bit Denisovan (usually less than 1 percent). People living in Melanesia (New Guinea and islands to the east) are as much as 5 percent Denisovan. This suggests that when humans reached Southeast Asia, possibly as early as 70,000 years ago, some of them interbred with a second population of Denisovans before moving on and settling Melanesia.

Some modern-day African and Asian populations also show faint traces of genetic mixing with a "ghost population." A ghost population means our genome carries evidence of interbreeding with an unknown hominin, although we haven't yet discovered any physical remains belonging to that species (such as bones). Scientists think Heidelbergensis evolved into three "sibling species" (humans, Neanderthals, and Denisovans), but perhaps there were other Heidelbergensis descendants that interbred with human groups.

One thing is clear: Moving and mixing is what humans do. It makes us who we are.

Although I'm sure that acquiring helpful genes wasn't on the minds of any humans, Neanderthals, Denisovans, or other hominins while they were (so to speak) mixing it up, interbreeding can offer evolutionary advantages. For example, we know from DNA analysis that the immune system of Neanderthals had evolved resistance to local diseases. When humans mated with them, the offspring that inherited Neanderthal genes for disease resistance were more likely to survive and reproduce.

Denisovan genes had advantages, too. Many modern-day Sherpas, who live at high altitudes in the Himalayas, have inherited "super-athlete" Denisovan genes that improve their ability to use oxygen in thin air. We know Denisovans lived at high altitudes because a 160,000-year-old Denisovan jawbone was found at 3,280 meters (10,800 feet) above sea level on the Tibetan Plateau in China.

By about 70,000 years ago, we reached Southeast Asia and began island-hopping. It's likely we constructed rafts to ferry ourselves across the water. Eventually we reached the island of Flores in Indonesia. It was here, perhaps, that we met Hobbits. If our ancestors gawked at burly Neanderthals and Denisovans, their eyes probably popped at the sight of *Homo floresiensis*.

An Indonesian scientist holds a cast of a Flores Hobbit skull.

Adult Flores Hobbits were about the height and weight of an eight-year-old human. They had stocky bodies with relatively long arms and long feet.[6] Despite their chimp-sized brains, the Hobbits controlled fire and used stone tools. They did not, however, live in snug Hobbit holes with round doors and cozy fireplaces. The Hobbits' world was a tropical forest inhabited by pygmy elephants and Komodo dragons.

If Flores sounds strange, all I can say is: just wait until we get to Australia.

The Flores Hobbits lived on Flores when the island was separated from the mainland by hundreds of kilometers of open water. A tsunami may have washed a group of Erectus (or possibly another hominin) out to sea, and

---

6   Did they have thick brown hair on the tops of those big feet? Nobody knows, but I certainly hope so.

the survivors clung to a raft of vegetation until they washed up on Flores. It's likely lizards also arrived via some kind of accidental ark. Elephants, being surprisingly good swimmers,[7] may have paddled over on their own.

Island environments often select for smaller individuals. That's because the smaller you are, the less food you need, and islands tend to have more limited food supplies than mainland environments. Scientists think this selection pressure caused the descendants of those first cast-aways to gradually downsize into Hobbits. Similar selection pressure caused the elephants to become pony sized.

Okay, but what about those supersized lizards?

On the Southeast Asian mainland, the role of big predator was filled by tigers and leopards. Big cats, however, never floated across to Flores. Evolution works with whatever is at hand, and what was at hand on Flores was a lizard. The Flores environment selected for bigger lizards because bigger ones were better able to take advantage of the island's deer, pigs, and pony-sized elephants. The Flores lizards upsized into Komodo dragons.

Here's a handy rule about evolution: weird things happen on islands.

Bones and teeth from a second Hobbit species (*Homo luzonensis*) have been found on Luzon Island in the Philippines. The Luzon Hobbit was slightly bigger than the Flores Hobbit and had curved finger and toe bones designed for tree climbing. We don't know if humans made it to Luzon before its Hobbits went extinct.

By about 65,000 years ago, we had island-hopped all the way to Australia. There we found kangaroos the size of horses, wombats the size of rhinos, and marsupial lions the size of, well, lions. Not to mention 6-meter (19-foot) lizards that could've eaten a Komodo dragon for

---

7   With a built-in snorkel.

breakfast. Plus *Genyornis newtoni*, last in a line of giant flightless birds nicknamed the "Demon Ducks of Doom."[8]

Another handy rule: weird things happen on isolated continents.

Let's pause at around 50,000 years ago. Humanity has spread eastward from Africa all the way to Australia. We aren't the only hominins around, but given the diverse habitats we live in, we're clearly the most adaptable. We've invented new technologies like javelins, arrows, chisels, barbed points for spearfishing, and bone needles for sewing skins into clothing or shelter.

Around 46,000 years ago, we finally reached Europe. The oldest human remains found there belong to a woman who lived in the Czech Republic (eastern Europe). From DNA analysis we know she was dark skinned, brown haired, and brown eyed, and had a Neanderthal ancestor seventy to eighty generations back.

You might wonder why it took so long to get to Europe, given that it's much closer to Africa than Australia. But Europe 46,000 years ago was a particularly challenging place to survive. When Heidelbergensis settled there about 450,000 years earlier, Europe was mostly forest. The Neanderthals—the descendants of European Heidelbergensis—were adapted to life in these woodlands. But when the last Ice Age arrived, temperatures fell. Ice sheets covered the north, and in the south the forests were replaced by treeless tundra. Neanderthals, despite their adaptations to the cold, struggled. It may have been difficult for many Neanderthal groups to adapt their forest style of hunting to confronting mammoths, wild horses, wild cattle, and woolly rhinos on Europe's open grasslands.

Enter us.

---

8   Kudos to those first Australians. I would've gotten back on my raft and paddled away. *Fast.*

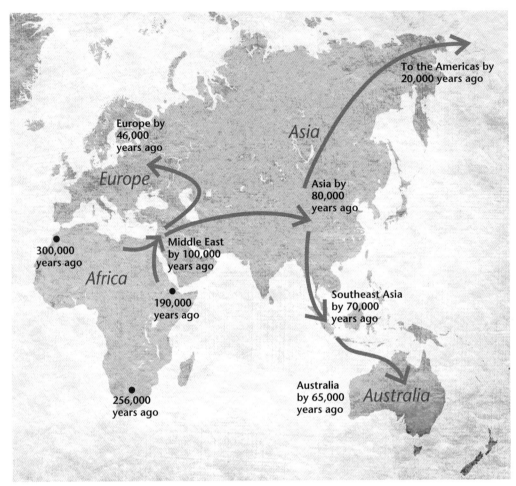

Major sites of early modern Homo sapiens *fossils in Africa, and human migration to major areas of the world. Modern coastlines are shown for clarity.*

Sure, the first modern humans to reach Europe had picked up some handy Neanderthal genes along the way, but humans evolved in Africa. Our bodies hadn't been selected for survival in cold environments. Our brains weren't bigger than those of the Neanderthals, so no obvious advantage there. And yet (spoiler alert) the Neanderthals died out and we didn't.

Our key advantage may have been collective brainpower. Collective brainpower is less about the size of our brains than the way we connect our brains together through communication and cooperation.

We know humans living in Ice Age Europe had trade networks. Certain types of stones and other materials (like seashells) are found only in certain places, so whenever they're discovered in sites many kilometers from their place of origin, we know trading was happening. And trading tells us different groups were coming together to share goods and ideas.

Of course, sometimes groups conflict. We're a clannish species, and we often separate ourselves into "us" versus "them" for the flimsiest of reasons. There's a college rivalry within my own family that is profoundly meaningless. Yet would I pass up an opportunity to promote my team?[9]

As clannish as we are, we are also intensely social. When we meet strangers and share goods and ideas, the benefits can be enormous. It works like this: Maybe someone's discovered a new medicinal plant, or invented a fish trap, or created a tool for punching holes in animal skins. A larger social network means more opportunities for the innovation to spread. There's less chance the new idea will be lost. As more people try out the innovation, it becomes more likely one of the users will improve on it. Perhaps the medicinal plant is more effective after heating it, or the fish trap works better if weighted with stones. Maybe someone adds a hole to the end of the hole-punching tool. Voilà: the world's first needle.

Innovation helped us overcome the challenges of Ice Age Europe, just as it helped us survive the challenges of Africa, Asia, and Australia. And the period beginning about 50,000 years ago is the first time undeniable evidence of complex symbolic communication appears. In other words: storytelling. Yes, it's been a long and winding journey, but we're finally circling back to *Star Wars*.

9   Of course not. GO BEARS!

Storytelling might seem like fluffy amusement. Sharp spears, warm bearskins, flints for fire-starting—those are useful things. Yet storytelling was an essential part of our success.

When you tell a story, you can replay events, imagine alternatives, and teach youngsters what to do and what not to do. *Remember when Org got gored? If he hadn't gone after the rhino calf alone . . .*

Even entirely fictional stories—sometimes *especially* fictional stories—give instructions about how to live. A story isn't a direct imitation of the real world. It's a simulation that highlights certain acts, or values, or ways of thinking. Heroes overcome adversity; they are brave and loyal and keep going even when all seems lost. Friends help each other. Evil must be fought. Themes found in *Star Wars* and *Harry Potter* are also found in *Gilgamesh*, the oldest surviving story in written form. Through stories we work out what matters. Through stories we share values and tell a collective tale about who we are and how we came to be. We are more likely to trust those who share our values. Trust enhances cooperation, and cooperation enhances survival.

It's true stories often involve people behaving badly. That shouldn't be surprising. To be effective, narrative must attract our attention, and there's nothing quite as attention getting as breaking a rule (Don't Kill, Don't Steal, Don't Mess with Darth Vader). We're social animals; social violations make our heads swivel. And while characters in stories often do terrible things, in most narratives the rule-breakers are caught and punished. The murderer is revealed, the liar unmasked, the wrong made right. Emperor Palpatine and Lord Voldemort are vanquished; moral order is restored. How immensely satisfying.

Remember theory of mind, which allows us to imagine what someone else might be thinking? Once you have a well-developed theory of mind, it's not much of a stretch to imagine a human-like mind behind lightning bolts or earthquakes. We can't control thunderstorms or shifts in the Earth's crust, but a story about battling gods places our fear within a framework we can understand. Explanations—including supernatural explanations—provide comfort and meaning. And if there's anything more riveting than *social* rule-breaking, it's breaking the laws of reality. That's why so many memorable stories feature gods, ghosts, demons, magic, and humans with superhuman powers.

A group of indigenous Australians tell a story about Budj Bim, an ancestral being who spat liquid fire from his teeth as he emerged from the earth. Budj Bim is also the name of the local volcano, which last erupted 37,000 years ago. This supernatural explanation of a natural disaster may be the world's oldest surviving tale, passed from generation to generation through oral tradition. That's 33,000 years before *Gilgamesh*.

And let's not forget that stories can let us see the world through another's eyes. (Here's theory of mind at work again.) We can get outside our own skin; we can explore what it's like to be an entirely different person living an entirely different life. Through stories we can experience a vast range of challenging situations and intense emotions without actually suffering from them. The best stories broaden our horizons, deepen our thinking, and spark our compassion. The best stories help us make better real-world decisions.

You might protest that a story is just a cheap thrill. Yes! That's the whole point. A story is the cheapest, most thrilling survival tool ever.

The oldest convincing evidence of storytelling comes to us from opposite ends of the world: Southeast Asia and western Europe. These stories slumbered for thousands of years before being rediscovered in modern times.

On the island of Sulawesi in Indonesia, 44,000 years ago, we painted the first story scene:

In Germany, about 40,000 years ago, we transformed a piece of mammoth ivory into this:

Around 34,000 years ago, we entered a cave in France and painted this:

About 16,000 years ago, in a different French cave, we painted this:

No one knows how to read these long-lost symbols and the stories they narrate. What's going on with that water buffalo surrounded by sort-of-human-sort-of-animal creatures? Are those lines spears, ropes, or rays of magic? Was "Lion Man" our first superhero? What's with the horse parade? The speared bull with its guts spilling out, that beak-nosed man falling backward . . . I'm not touching *that* with a ten-foot pole. Even though there's a ten-foot pole in the picture.

And is that rhino the first art critic? Ouch.

One thing is certain: whether or not we understand these symbols, it's obvious these works were created by people with complex mental, spiritual, and emotional lives. In every way that truly matters, they are us.

I think it's safe to say that if we went back in time, these people would understand a prehistoric version of *Star Wars*. Or Homer's *Odyssey*. Or Shakespeare's *Romeo and Juliet*.[10] Though I'm not sure I could ever explain *SpongeBob SquarePants*.

---

10   With a Neanderthal Romeo and a human Juliet, of course.

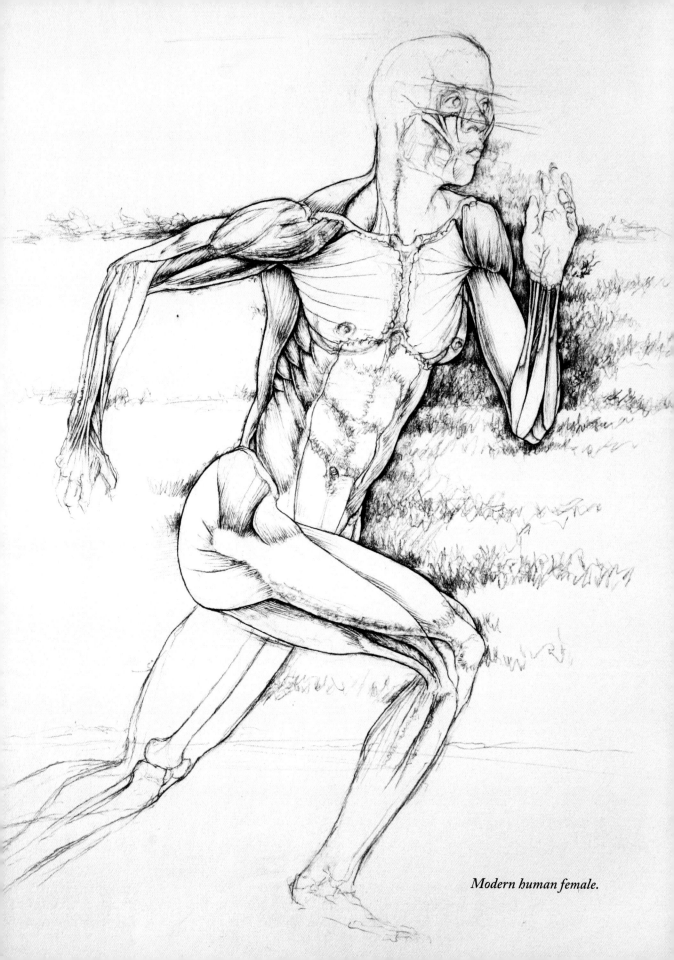

Modern human female.

CONCLUSION
WE DOMINATE

"People often find it easier to be a result of the past than a cause of the future."

—Anonymous

This part makes me think of *The Lord of the Rings*, when the Age of Men dawns and the Elves depart Middle-earth forever. Except in our case the Orcs, Hobbits, Dwarves, and Ents also take their leave. In other words: all the other hominins go extinct.

Erectus was the first to exit. Our ancestor species had long ago disappeared from Africa and mainland Asia, but until about 110,000 years ago, a population survived on the island of Java in Southeast Asia. As you may recall, evolution moves at different speeds in different places. If a habitat is stable and selection pressure is minimal, a population might not change much, even after hundreds of thousands of years. So it was with Erectus. But at last they dwindled and disappeared, possibly due to climate changes.

The Hobbits were next. The Luzon Hobbits died out by 50,000 years ago. We don't know what caused their disappearance. Extinction isn't usually the result of a grand event like the meteor that took down the dinosaurs. More often it's a series of little shoves. A vulnerable species gets pushed closer and closer to the edge of oblivion until it finally topples over.

In the case of the Flores Hobbits, however, there was a dramatic event. The Flores Hobbits and the pygmy elephants vanished in the wake of a volcanic eruption on Flores about 50,000 years ago. A small number of Komodo dragons still survive on the island.

The Neanderthals departed by about 40,000 years ago. There's a lot of debate about why. They were never very numerous, and when the Neanderthals were forced south during the Ice Age, their numbers likely dropped even lower. Small, isolated populations are more vulnerable to extinction. The loss of essential skills is also more likely in small and isolated groups. If your best spear-maker dies without having taught an apprentice, the next generation of spears won't be as good.

Many different little shoves could've pushed the Neanderthals to the edge: massive volcanic eruptions in Europe that obscured the sun and made the climate even colder; a lack of game due to these and other climate changes; new diseases brought by arriving humans; and competition with humans for food and other resources. While some speculate that we deliberately killed off our cousins, there's no evidence of that. Perhaps a dwindling number of Neanderthals were simply absorbed into local human groups.

It appears the Denisovans were the last hominin to share the planet with us. The only Denisovan fossils we possess are scattered bits of bone and teeth from a cave in Siberia, a jawbone from the Tibetan Plateau in China, and a skull found in China that may be Denisovan. The most recent remains are at least 52,000 years old. But by analyzing the genome of modern people from Southeast Asia and New Guinea, scientists discovered evidence of human-Denisovan interbreeding as late as 15,000 years ago. The mixing probably happened in Southeast Asia.

The Erectus, Hobbits, Neanderthals, and Denisovans who were the last of their kind probably didn't understand what was happening. At least I hope they didn't. Maybe they imagined there were others like them living in the next valley.

After the extinction of the Denisovans, we were alone.

We had never before been the only hominin around. Heidelbergensis hadn't been alone. Or Erectus, or the Handy People, or the Australopiths. The earliest upright walkers—Sahel, Orrorin, and Kadabba—probably weren't alone, either. Being Earth's only hominin is terribly sad. Like going to a family reunion and finding nobody there.

I'm going to skip through the last 30,000 years very quickly. I know this is just one of many stories you'll encounter throughout your day, whether it's in the form of a novel or a social-media post or a video game.[1] But this story is about you. And everyone you will ever meet.

We kept on exploring. More than 20,000 years ago—possibly as early as 30,000 years ago—some of us left Siberia and discovered the Americas. It was a new world of dire wolves, cheetahs, saber-tooth cats, giant ground sloths, camels, mammoths, and mastodons.

Around 19,000 years ago, the world started to become warmer and wetter. As the ice sheets retreated, great tracts of land in the Northern Hemisphere became habitable. Our numbers increased.

As our population grew, so did our social networks. Innovations spread. Cultural evolution, rather than biological evolution, became the driving force in our existence. By about 11,000 years ago, agriculture appeared in both the Middle East and Asia. Around 6,000 years ago, in Mesopotamia (modern Syria and Iraq), we built our first cities. Once we lived in cities, where large numbers of people interconnect, innovation ramped up. Writing appeared about 5,400 years ago in Mesopotamia, and shortly afterward

---

1   Not to be judgmental, but given the value of storytelling, I hope it's an RPG.

(probably independently) in China. Population growth in the Americas also led to the independent invention of agriculture, cities, and writing.

Today cultural evolution has gone into hyperdrive. Innovation now operates at such a frantic pace I've had to think hard about using words like *hashtag* or *video game*. In a few years they might be as obsolete as VCRs.[2] In 1829, when the first Neanderthal fossil was discovered, no one knew what it was or what it meant. Now a pinch of powdered bone from a Neanderthal can tell us not just that we are related to her and by how much, but also that she was a redhead.

On the other hand, emoji poetry was invented in 2012. So we're capable of moving backward.[3]

We can now imagine futuristic technologies that may allow us to visit other planets. Perhaps someday we'll be the alien scientists judging the braininess of creatures on another world.[4]

Our prehistoric environments gave us big brains. Today we use our big brains to tailor our environment to our needs. Or at least our short-term needs. Over the past 10,000 years, we've transformed natural ecosystems to such an extent that three-fourths of all land environments are now of our making: cities, towns, factories, agricultural land, and land for domestic animals.

I'll spare you a multitude of facts and figures in favor of a few mind-games.

Imagine stacking all the domestic birds on Earth (mostly chickens) in one big squawking, screeching, feathery pile. Make another pile of every wild

---

2   Your grandparents owned these but never figured out how to program them.

3   I'm ! Don't send me emojis.

4   But hopefully we won't haul them back and put them on display in a zoo or aquarium. In fact, we might want to stop doing this to dolphins.

bird on the planet—every pigeon, every sparrow, every eagle, down to the last hummingbird. The mass of domestic birds would be *three times* bigger.

Or . . . squish together every one of the 7.8 billion humans along with all of the mammals we keep as livestock (cattle, pigs, etc.). Compare this uncomfortable lump to an equally uncomfortable lump of every wild mammal on the planet. Every elephant, every bear, every kangaroo, everything down to the last little mouse. The pile of us and our livestock would be *twenty-two times* bigger.

Between 1970 and 2016, populations of wild birds, mammals, amphibians, reptiles, and fish declined, on average, by 68 percent. Since we started building cities and plowing land, so many species have gone extinct that if we reversed the trend tomorrow, it would take 5 to 7 million years of evolution to regain the lost diversity.

I'm not trying to make you curl into a fetal position to await the end of the world. But we need to take responsibility for our planetary impacts. Our overuse of fossil fuels is driving a drastic long-term change in our climate that is not going to make Earth a nicer place.

I'm hopeful we can turn things around. We're a super-smart species, yes. But it's not just our mental abilities that make us dominant. It's our extraordinary ability to cooperate. Of course, social insects like ants and bees are also extremely cooperative. But ants and bees don't have computers and cruise missiles.[5]

Our ability to cooperate has made possible every great shrine, cathedral, mosque, and temple ever built, as well as every religious war ever fought. Without cooperation the Holocaust would never have happened. Without cooperation we would never have eradicated smallpox.

---

5   And let's hope they never acquire them. Against the Bee Borg, resistance would be futile.

We have the potential to cooperate on climate change. We can do something about that and every other form of environmental degradation from overfishing to strip mining. Not to mention all the non-environmental problems we face. We have the potential, you and I, to do better. We inherited that potential from all those Australopiths, Handy People, Erectus, Heidelbergensis, and ancient *Homo sapiens* who lived and struggled and died. They made us. We owe them our best effort.

Let's return to our distant past. Around 40,000 years ago, on the island of Sulawesi in Indonesia, someone pressed their hand against the wall of a cave. Using their mouth, or possibly a tube, they blew an ochre mixture around their hand.

Later, in a cave in Spain, someone else did the same.

People in Australia did it, too.

So did people in Africa . . .

And so did the first Americans.

When did we become human? Was it when we stood up, or when we made the first stone tool? Did we become human when we explored the world? Was it when we mastered fire, or when we mastered our vocal cords? Did we become human when we told our first story?

I hope by now you see that being human isn't one thing. It's a constellation of abilities. Each helped make us possible.

So please take one final look at those hand stencils. The people who made those images never met. They were separated by thousands of kilometers of forest, desert, savanna, mountain, jungle, and ocean. They would not have spoken the same language, eaten the same foods, or dressed in the same clothing. They would not have told the same stories. Yet these ghostly hands tell us something important.

We are one. One species. What unites us lies deeper than what divides us.

Author's Notes

A Note on Race

You might have noticed that although this book is about human evolution, I have not once mentioned race. That's because race is a cultural concept, not a biological reality. That doesn't mean race doesn't exist. It does exist, and it plays an outsized role in today's society—sometimes obviously, sometimes less obviously. But race isn't about DNA.

Race is a way of classifying people that is used by those in a position of power (most often white people of European descent) to justify oppression and discrimination. And while humans have always created group identities that separate "us" from "them," racism goes further: it labels some people not just as "other" but also as "less than human."

The modern concept of race is relatively recent. It is tied to efforts by early European scientists and naturalists to arrange life on a religiously inspired ladder with the Christian God at the top, followed by angels, then white people, with other races just a step above monkeys and apes. These racial concepts were closely tied to the wave of European colonialism that began in the sixteenth century.

Racism continues to exist and continues to impact how we relate to one another. Some of the impacts of race and racism are social (unequal access to justice, jobs, housing, education, and health care). Others are biological (higher rates of illness and death due to the social impacts of racism).

But aren't there genetic variations between human populations? Well, yes. Most of our genetic diversity can be found on one continent: Africa.

That's because everyone living *outside* Africa descends from a subset of Africans who left Africa.

Okay, but haven't some genetic differences sprung up since some people left Africa? Yes. As I hope you've learned from this book, different environments (physical or social) create different selection pressures. But most variations don't align with race. Instead they align with where people live and how they make a living.

The evolution of lactose tolerance is one example. All mammals can digest lactose (a sugar found in milk) when they are babies, but the gene that allows them to digest lactose is turned off as the animal matures. And so it was, originally, with all of us. But during the last 10,000 years, lactose tolerance has evolved independently in at least five different parts of the world. In each of these places, people kept milk-producing livestock such as cattle, horses, sheep, and goats.

Through random variation, a few people were born with a gene for digesting lactose that never turned off. These individuals could drink milk throughout their life. If you've got livestock and lifelong lactose tolerance, you've got steady access to high-quality protein. The lactose tolerant were more likely to survive the hard times, and so were those offspring who inherited the trait. This useful genetic variation spread through these livestock-keeping populations. Milk was the gift that kept on giving.

Lactose tolerance evolved among livestock herders in northern Europe, northern Asia, North Africa, West Africa, and East Africa. It's based on environmental and social conditions and has nothing to do with race.

What about sickle cell anemia? Sickle cell anemia is a genetic blood disease often associated with people of African descent, particularly African Americans whose ancestors were enslaved and brought to the United States from West Africa. Many people assume the disease is linked to race, but a person doesn't carry the sickle cell trait because they are Black. The sickle cell trait is found in people who descend from Africans who were both farmers (most commonly West African farmers) and who were regularly exposed to malaria. Farmers tend to live settled lives, and farming tends to create environments (ditches, small pools of water) that provide places for malaria-carrying mosquitoes to breed. The sickle cell trait protects against malaria, so in its original context, it offered survival benefits that outweighed its costs. Sickle cell anemia is rare among the Maasai people of East Africa, who are nomadic and live in dry, higher-altitude areas.[1] And in some places in southern Europe and South Asia where malaria is a problem, there are also high rates of sickle cell anemia. Skin color doesn't enter into it.

Don't forget: human populations aren't static. In historical times the rise and fall of empires, the trafficking of enslaved peoples, and colonialism have resulted in the remixing of long-separated populations. And as I hope you've learned from this book, we humans have been moving and mixing and mating with other groups ever since we've been on the planet. That includes mating (now and then) with other kinds of hominins. "Racial purity" is a myth. Even "species purity" is a myth.

Still, you might insist, there are noticeable physical differences between people from different parts of the globe. Ask yourself: What would visiting alien scientists think of those variations? I suspect they would find our differences no more remarkable than the fur color differences among wolves. We humans are primates: highly visual, highly social creatures. We are biased toward visual information, and we evolved to pay especially close attention to other people's faces. That bias makes small physical

---

1   And by the way, Maasai, who drink cow's milk, are as lactose tolerant as Germans.

differences seem more significant than they actually are. Racism harnesses and exaggerates that bias.[2]

Although race isn't a scientifically useful way of thinking about human genetic diversity, that doesn't mean science is free from racial bias. To grow up in a society is to absorb its prejudices. There's no vaccination that gives scientists immunity from racism. In the nineteenth century, the eugenics movement promoted the false notion that preventing "undesirables" such as non-white people from reproducing would "improve" humanity. It's just one example of how science (or pseudoscience) has been used to promote racism.

What scientists *can* do is use their most powerful tools—rationality and evidence—to document how racism impacts human health and well-being. Studies of implicit racial bias, in particular, can help us understand how to counteract it. Scientists can also acknowledge the implicit racial bias within the science community and strive to minimize its effect on their work and in their workplaces. As Tyrone Hayes, Professor of Integrative Biology at the University of California, Berkeley, reminds his fellow scientists: "Remember that antiracism and fighting racism starts at home."

MORE ON EVOLUTION

Although natural selection is the main "engine" of evolution, there are other ways evolution occurs. These other evolutionary processes include sexual selection (which is actually a special subcategory of natural selection involving mate choice), genetic drift, horizontal gene transfer, and *de novo* changes to the genome.

---

2   If wolves discriminated against other wolves, it would probably be on the basis of smell. If dolphins discriminated against other dolphins, it would probably be based on information received through echolocation. But I like to think wolves and dolphins are better than that.

Sexual selection happens when the "choosier" sex (often the female) decides on a mate based on qualities that—on first glance, at least—don't seem to have anything to do with evolutionary fitness. Sexual selection has produced oddities such as the male peacock's ridiculously cumbersome tail. On second glance, however, sexual selection is weirdly practical. If you're a male peacock, you need to be in great physical shape (well-fed, no disease, etc.) in order to grow those lavishly unnecessary feathers. *It's not just a tail; it's a sign of my underlying awesomeness. Pick me, babe!*

Genetic drift is in some ways the complete opposite of natural selection. Natural selection is NON-random (hence the word *selection*), but genetic drift happens when a completely random event impacts a species' evolution. Genetic drift is most common in small populations.

Let's say a half dozen deer swim from a larger island to a smaller one. The larger island has a volcano that erupts and wipes out all the deer on that island. All future deer of that species will now descend solely from those half dozen deer that happened to live on the smaller island. Any genetic variations not present in those original half dozen deer have been lost—not because those variations weren't selected, but because they were randomly eliminated. This is evolution by way of genetic drift. (When I think of genetic drift, I imagine survivors . . . on a raft . . . drifting on a current . . .)

Horizontal gene transfer is a new evolutionary wrinkle, very science-fiction-y and cutting-edge. Scientists have found evidence of genes that transferred directly between species—sometimes between species that are very, very distantly related.

Normally, genes move vertically over time, from a parent organism to its offspring. In horizontal gene transfer, bits of genetic material transfer from one organism into an entirely different kind of organism. For example, scientists have found genes in humans that were clearly acquired from microorganisms through horizontal gene transfer. Does horizontal gene transfer have a large, middling, or minor impact on the course of evolution? No one yet knows.

***De novo* genetic change** is even more science-fiction-y than gene transfer. *De novo* evolution involves "junk" DNA. Junk DNA are stretches within our genome that don't seem to code for anything. In *de novo* evolution, bits of this junk DNA self-assemble into working genes. It's as if you opened the kitchen junk drawer and discovered that an odd spoon and a bent fork had assembled themselves into salad tongs.

The kind of cod served up in fish-and-chips has an antifreeze in its blood that keeps the fish from freezing in Arctic waters. The gene coding for this seems to have arisen from junk DNA (which turns out not to be quite so junky after all). *De novo* genetic change isn't yet well understood, to say the least.

Evolution means the POPULATION changes over time—NOT the individual. We need to be more precise about how we talk about evolution. When someone says something like "the mountain gorilla adapted to life in cool, high-altitude forests by growing a thicker coat of fur," it sounds as if a savvy mountain gorilla decided to grow its hair out. NO. An individual mountain gorilla lives or dies with whatever fur thickness is encoded in its genes. If thicker hair has a positive impact on survival and reproduction, then generation after generation, genes for thicker hair will tend to spread through the mountain gorilla population. In evolution by natural selection, the *population*, not the individual, adapts to its environment.

Evolution doesn't offer moral values. Some people imagine that because evolution through natural selection is "natural," the notion of "survival of the fittest" should be used as a model of how to run human society. (I'm sure it's just a coincidence that those who promote this idea always assume they're among the "fittest.")

Natural doesn't necessarily mean "good" or "desirable." In early human societies it was entirely natural for half of all children to die of disease and malnutrition and for most adults to expire before they reached forty. Does anybody think that's how we should run a hospital?

Evolution through natural selection is neither moral nor immoral. It's as unrelated to morality as gravity, or magnetism, or any other natural force. As it turns out, the natural process of evolution did equip us with brains capable of making moral decisions and determining how to create a good society.

Evolution is not about progress or perfection. Evolution has no particular goal. No end game. Just as the piece of Earth's crust that rear-ended Asia didn't intend to create the Himalayas, evolution didn't intend to create us. The tree of life really is a big bushy tree, not a ladder with us perched triumphantly on the top rung. Evolution produced us, but it isn't *about* us. We lived and struggled and died, and we've been lucky. Unlike the dinosaurs, we haven't had to cope with a planet-altering disaster.[3]

Even though evolution isn't striving for progress or perfection, its creative power remains astonishing. Charles Darwin, the first scientist to grasp how evolution works, marveled at the diversity of the big bushy tree of life. "Whilst this planet has gone cycling on according to the fixed laws of gravity," he wrote, "from so simple a beginning endless forms most beautiful and most wonderful have been, and are being, evolved."[4]

---

3   Though between climate change and our consumption of wild animals (which allows novel viruses to jump to human populations), we're working on it.

4   This would be a good time to do an internet search for mandarin fish, golden pheasants, and sea slugs. *Especially* sea slugs.

More about Dating Fossils, Artifacts, and Climate Shifts

Fossils are the remains of living things that died long ago. Bones and teeth are the hardest parts of an animal's body and therefore the most likely to last long enough to end up in a museum display. Fossils are often dated by calculating the age of the geological layer in which they are found. For example, some minerals created by volcanic eruptions contain radioactive substances that decay at known rates. By identifying these radioactive layers, and noting whether the fossil was found above, below, or between radioactive layers, a scientist can calculate a date range for the fossil.

An adult male Neanderthal from Israel (the Middle East). Scientists used radioactive dating techniques to determine that he lived about 60,000 years ago.

In some cases, a fossil can be dated if it's found alongside the fossils of species with better-known dates. A hominin fossil found alongside hyena bones is probably no older and no younger than the known date range for that hyena species.

Sometimes younger fossils can be dated directly. As an animal or plant grows, its tissues take up a special form of carbon known as carbon-14. When the animal dies, the carbon-14 in its tissues begins to decay. Fossils up to about 60,000 years old can be dated by this radiocarbon technique. Older fossils have lost so much carbon-14 that it can no longer be detected.

What about artifacts such as tools and jewelry? Often these are dated in the same way as fossils: by determining the age of the geologic layer in which they are found. If the artifact is biological, such as a wooden spear-shaft, radiocarbon dating may be used to date the wood. The age of cave paintings may be dated by sampling the age of a small bit of the charcoal used to make the painting. Sometimes cave paintings have become partially covered by calcite deposits, which can be dated by the radioactive decay of small quantities of uranium in the calcite. For example, if a calcite deposit on top of a painting is 40,000 years old, the painting underneath can't be any younger.

"Molecular clocks" are an interesting way of dating when different species emerged. All animals have certain molecules that mutate (change) at a regular rate. By comparing the structure of these molecules in two animals of different species, scientists can estimate when they last shared a common ancestor.

DNA analysis can give us a much more detailed idea about how two species are related. Currently, DNA from 400,000-year-old hominins has been successfully extracted and analyzed. Perhaps even older bones will yield secrets as technology improves.

The newest approach to studying the relationships between long-dead species is the field of proteomics, in which ancient proteins are analyzed and compared between species. Because proteins are sturdier than DNA, it's possible to use this technology on fossils that no longer contain any detectible DNA. Protein analysis has been used successfully on a 1.9-million-year-old "Wookiee" tooth (the *Gigantopithecus blacki* mentioned on page 52) to show the species is related to modern orangutans. The technique is sure to lead to important new information about our ancient ancestors.

As you know from reading this book, a seesawing climate probably had a lot to do with human evolution. Scientists study ancient climates by studying the tell-tale markers climate changes leave behind in lake and ocean sediments, glaciers and ice sheets, tree rings, corals, and cave formations. The presence or absence of different kinds of fossilized plants (including seeds and pollens) and fossilized animals also suggests something about the climate in which they lived. And the balance of chemicals in ancient bones can be used to infer diet. Diet is determined by habitat, and habitat is determined by climate.

There's still so much we don't know about ancient hominins and the worlds in which they lived. We need more fossil finds and more technologies to enlighten us. I hope some of you who are reading this book will make contributions to the study of human evolution through your own amazing discoveries.

GLOSSARY

Acheulean tools: Originating about 1.8 million years ago, these tools were flaked on both sides, usually into a teardrop shape.

Cooking hypothesis: A proposed explanation of the impact of cooking on early human evolution put forth by scientist Richard Wrangham.

DNA: Short for *deoxyribonucleic acid*, DNA is a self-replicating molecule that encodes an organism's genetic information.

Evolution: The change in populations of living organisms over time.

Extractive foragers: Species that survive by finding ways to get at nutritious but hard-to-access foodstuffs.

Fossil: The preserved remains of a once-living organism.

FOXP2: A gene that seems to influence language ability.

Gaze signaling: The ability to direct another person's attention through eye movements.

Gene: A specific segment of DNA that serves as a unit of heredity. Often a gene is the recipe for making a specific protein.

Genetic diversity: The total of all the different genes in a population.

Genetic trait: Any feature of an organism expressed through its genes.

Genome: The full set of genes carried by an organism.

Ghost population: A population for which there is genetic evidence but no other physical evidence such as fossilized remains.

Great apes: The larger species of ape. The living great apes are orangutans, gorillas, chimpanzees, bonobos, and humans.

Hominins: Humans and all species ancestral to humans, as well as our extinct close relatives since our last common ancestor with chimpanzees and bonobos. "Hominin" is, not surprisingly, often confused with the term "hominid." A hominid includes both hominins and all of their great ape relatives, living and extinct, including *Gigantopithecus blacki* (the extinct Wookiee) and modern bonobos, chimpanzees, gorillas, and orangutans.

Hybrid: An organism that results from the interbreeding of two closely related species.

Hyoid bone: A slender, curved bone in the throat that connects to ligaments and muscles and is important for human speech.

Hypothesis: A tentative conclusion or proposed explanation based on evidence.

Immune system: The biological network of cells, tissues, and organs that helps an organism fight disease.

Lomekwian tools: The very earliest stone tools (3.3 million years ago), named after their discovery site in Lomekwi, Kenya.

Mammals: A scientific subcategory of vertebrates (animals with backbones). All mammals have fur or hair and nourish young with milk.

Natural selection: The process of environmental pressures that result in differences in reproduction; over time, the most useful inherited traits spread through the population. Natural selection is considered the main driver of evolution.

Ochre: A natural mineral found in a wide range of earthy colors from yellow to deep reddish brown.

Oldowan tools: A very early (beginning 2.6 million years ago) tool technology consisting of simple choppers, scrapers, and pounders.

Primates: The subcategory of mammals that includes monkeys, apes, lemurs, lorises, and tarsiers.

Rift valley: A depression in the landscape, often with steep sides, created within a large zone of geological faults along a lengthy section of the Earth's crust.

Savanna: A grassland in the tropic or subtropic regions.

Sclera: The white part of the human eyeball.

Speciation: The formation of new species through the process of evolution.

Symbol: Something that represents something else.

Symbolic communication: Transmitting information indirectly through symbols.

Teaching (scientific definition): A way of transferring skills from one individual to another, in which the teacher varies their behavior in a way that costs the teacher but benefits the learner.

Theory (scientific definition): A well-thought-out, well-accepted explanation for a wide range of facts and observations. A scientific theory has proven predictive power, has been repeatedly confirmed through both experimentation and observation, and inspires new research and observations.

Tool (scientific definition): An unattached object used to manipulate something else.

Tubers: The parts of some plants that store nutrients underground.

TIME LINE

7 TO 5.2 MILLION YEARS AGO: First hominins (Sahel, Orrorin, and Kadabba). Signs of upright posture.

4.5 MILLION YEARS AGO: Ardi (*Ardipithecus ramidus*). Definitely upright.

4.2 MILLION YEARS AGO: Earliest Australopith.

3.4 MILLION YEARS AGO: Cut marks on bones; earliest evidence of hominin tool use.

3.3 MILLION YEARS AGO: Earliest known stone tools (Lomekwian).

3.2 MILLION YEARS AGO: Lucy (*Australopithecus afarensis*).

3 MILLION YEARS AGO: Makapansgat Pebble is carried to a site where Australopiths lived.

2.6 MILLION YEARS AGO: Earliest Oldowan tools.

2.4 MILLION YEARS AGO: Earliest Handy People.

2 MILLION YEARS AGO: Earliest Erectus. (Nariokotome Boy, the most famous specimen of Erectus, is 1.6 million years old.)

1.8 MILLION YEARS AGO: First Acheulean handaxes. Erectus in eastern Europe are the first known hominins to live outside Africa.

1.6 MILLION YEARS AGO: First evidence of hominin use of fire. Handy People become extinct around this time.

1.5 MILLION YEARS AGO: Erectus reaches Southeast Asia.

1.2 MILLION YEARS AGO: By this date all Australopiths (including robust Australopiths) are extinct.

700,000 YEARS AGO: Earliest Heidelbergensis. Earliest Flores Hobbit. Evidence (in Israel) of cooking and tended hearths.

500,000 YEARS AGO: Erectus engraves a mussel shell in Southeast Asia.

430,000 YEARS AGO: Earliest Neanderthals.

400,000 YEARS AGO: Earliest Denisovans. Regular use of fire.

300,000 YEARS AGO: Earliest *Homo sapiens*; first spears (made by Neanderthals).

200,000 YEARS AGO: First anatomically modern *Homo sapiens*. First migration out of Africa into southern Europe and the Middle East. These first migrants all appear to die out.

176,500 YEARS AGO: Neanderthals make stalagmite circles—possibly symbolic—deep inside a cave in Europe.

135,000 YEARS AGO: First shell beads, in North Africa and the Middle East.

110,000 YEARS AGO: Erectus becomes extinct.

100,000 YEARS AGO: *Homo sapiens* leaves Africa for the second time. Some *Homo sapiens* mate with Neanderthals in the Middle East.

80,000 YEARS AGO: In Asia some *Homo sapiens* mate with Denisovans.

70,000 YEARS AGO: *Homo sapiens* reaches Southeast Asia.

67,000 YEARS AGO: Earliest Luzon Hobbits.

65,000 YEARS AGO: *Homo sapiens* reaches Australia.

64,000 YEARS AGO: First cave painting; Neanderthals decorate a cave in Spain.

50,000 YEARS AGO: Flores Hobbits and Luzon Hobbits become extinct.

46,000 YEARS AGO: *Homo sapiens* reaches Europe.

44,000 YEARS AGO: First artwork depicting a story is painted in Leang Bulu' Sipong Cave 4 in Southeast Asia.

40,000 YEARS AGO: Neanderthals become extinct. "Lion Man" statue is carved in Europe.

34,000 YEARS AGO: Chauvet Cave is painted in Europe.

20,000 YEARS AGO: *Homo sapiens* reaches the Americas.

16,000 YEARS AGO: Lascaux Cave "Shaft Scene" is painted in Europe.

15,000 YEARS AGO: Denisovans become extinct. *Homo sapiens* becomes the only hominin species on Earth.

A More Complete List of the Hominin Family

Scientists often differ about how to interpret the fossil record. A cluster of bones might represent a distinct species or normal variation within a species. After all, individuals of any species will vary in size and shape. Some scientists are "splitters" and prefer to make fine distinctions between fossil specimens—which often means giving a specimen a unique species name. Other scientists are "lumpers." Lumpers prefer to classify specimens into a smaller number of species.

I've sided with the lumpers. I want you, my reader, to focus on the overall scope of human evolution rather than juggling dozens of species names. Fewer characters means it's easier to follow the plot.

In case you hear of a hominin species I haven't mentioned in this text, I've compiled a list of many of the species names you might come across in other books about human evolution. The species in bold are discussed in *How to Build a Human*.

Very Early Hominins
***Sahelanthropus tchadensis* ("Sahel"): 7 to 6 million years ago, north-central Africa.**
***Orrorin tugenensis* ("Orrorin"): 6.2 to 5.6 million years ago, East Africa.**

Ardipithecus Hominins
***Ardipithecus kadabba* ("Kadabba"): 5.8 to 5.2 million years ago, East Africa.**
***Ardipithecus ramidus* ("Ardi"): 4.5 to 4.3 million years ago, East Africa.**

Australopith Hominins
Australopithecus anamensis: 4.2 to 3.8 million years ago, East Africa.
Australopithecus bahrelghazali: 3.6 to 3 million years ago, north-central Africa.

Australopithecus afarensis ("Lucy"): **3.7 to 3 million years ago, East Africa.**
Australopithecus africanus: **3.3 to 2 million years ago, southern Africa.**
Australopithecus sediba: 2 million years ago, southern Africa.

HARD-TO-FIGURE-OUT HOMININ
Unfortunately, only a single, damaged skull has been uncovered. Some scientists think this is a distinct species. Others believe it's a specimen of *Australopithecus africanus*.

Kenyanthropus platyops: 3.5 to 3.3 million years ago, East Africa.

ROBUST AUSTRALOPITH HOMININS
These species are generally referred to as "robust Australopiths" because of their stockier bodies and heavy teeth and jaws.

Paranthropus aethiopicus: 2.7 to 2.3 million years ago, East Africa.
Australopithecus garhi: 2.5 to 2.3 million years ago, East Africa.
Paranthropus boisei: 2.3 to 1.4 million years ago, East Africa.
Paranthropus robustus: 2.1 to 1.2 million years ago, southern Africa.

HABILIS HOMININS
Homo rudolfensis is known from a single fossil skull. While some scientists think it's a variation of *Homo habilis*, others argue it should be a separate species based on its larger brain and flatter face. It might be a descendant of the hard-to-figure-out *Kenyanthropus platyops*.

Homo habilis ("Handy People"): **2.4 to 1.6 million years ago, East Africa, southern Africa.**
Homo rudolfensis: 1.9 million years ago, East Africa.

ERECTUS HOMININS
While some scientists would group all of these under *Homo erectus*, others think older fossils from Central Europe and Africa should have their own species label.

Homo georgicus: 1.8 million years ago, Central Europe.
Homo ergaster: 1.9 to 1.5 million years ago, East Africa.
Homo erectus ("Erectus"; also "Nariokotome Boy"): **2 million years ago to 110,000 years ago, Africa, Asia, eastern Europe.**

YET ANOTHER HARD-TO-FIGURE-OUT HOMININ

Some scientists think a group of fossils found in Spain are a distinct species and should have a distinct name. Others think the specimens should be considered either *Homo erectus* or *Homo heidelbergensis.*

Homo antecessor: 1.2 million to 780,000 years ago, Europe.

HOBBIT HOMININS

Homo floresiensis ("Flores Hobbit"): **700,000 to 50,000 years ago, Southeast Asia.**
Homo luzonensis ("Luzon Hobbit"): **67,000 to 50,000 years ago, Southeast Asia.**

HEIDELBERGENSIS HOMININ

Homo heidelbergensis ("Heidelbergensis"): **700,000 to 200,000 years ago, Africa, Asia, Europe.**

AND YET ANOTHER HARD-TO-FIGURE-OUT HOMININ

This one is almost as quirky as the Hobbits. Some of its features (chimp-sized brain, shoulders, rib cage) resemble an Australopith's, while others (hands and feet) are closer to a modern human's. It might have overlapped (just barely) with early *Homo sapiens.*

Homo naledi: 335,000 to 236,000 years ago, southern Africa.

HUMANS AND OUR SIBLING SPECIES

Homo neanderthalensis ("Neanderthal"): **430,000 to 40,000 years ago, Europe, Middle East, central Asia.**
Denisovans: **400,000 to 15,000 years ago, central Asia; probably also Southeast Asia. (The Denisovans do not yet have an official species name.)**
Homo sapiens: **(go look in a mirror): 300,000 years ago to present, just about everywhere on Earth. A few of us have even made it to the Moon.**

Recommended Books and Websites

Recommended Reading

Berger, Lee R., and Marc Aronson. *The Skull in the Rock: How a Scientist, a Boy, and Google Earth Opened a New Window on Human Origins.* Washington, DC: National Geographic, 2012.

Coyne, Jerry A. *Why Evolution Is True.* New York: Penguin, 2010.

Diamond, Jared. *The Third Chimpanzee for Young People: On the Evolution and Future of the Human Animal.* New York: Seven Stories Press, 2014.

Potts, Richard, and Christopher Sloan. *What Does It Mean to Be Human?* Washington, DC: National Geographic, 2010.

Roberts, Alice. *Evolution: The Human Story.* 2nd ed. New York: DK, 2018.

Thimmesh, Catherine. *Lucy Long Ago: Uncovering the Mystery of Where We Came From.* Boston: Houghton Mifflin Harcourt, 2009.

Online Resources

"The Anne and Bernard Spitzer Hall of Human Origins," American Museum of Natural History: https://www.amnh.org/exhibitions/permanent-exhibitions/anne-and-bernard-spitzer-hall-of-human-origins

"Charles Darwin: A Gentle Revolutionary," The Story Behind the Science: https://www.storybehindthescience.org/pdf/darwin.pdf

"Climate Effects on Human Evolution," Smithsonian National Museum of Natural History: http://humanorigins.si.edu/research/climate-and-human-evolution/climate-effects-human-evolution

"Human Evolution Interactive Timeline," Smithsonian National Museum of Natural History: http://humanorigins.si.edu/evidence/human-evolution-interactive-timeline

"Race and Human Variation," American Anthropological Association: https://understandingrace.org/RaceAndHumanVariation

"Seven Million Years of Human Evolution," American Museum of Natural History: https://www.youtube.com/watch?v=DZv8VyIQ7YU

"Understanding Evolution," University of California Museum of Paleontology and the National Center for Science Education: https://evolution.berkeley.edu/evolibrary/article/evo_01

"What Does It Mean to Be Human?" Smithsonian National Museum of Natural History: http://humanorigins.si.edu/

ACKNOWLEDGMENTS

I'm immensely grateful to biological anthropologist Habiba Chirchir, Associate Professor of Biological Sciences at Marshall University, and paleoanthropologist Richard Potts, Director of the Human Origins Program at the Smithsonian Institution, who despite dauntingly busy schedules reviewed my manuscript and provided both encouragement and invaluable comments. Dr. Chirchir also very kindly contributed a foreword and a cultural sensitivity review. I feel incredibly lucky that paleoartist John Gurche lent his stunning artwork to this book. His art brings us close to our ancient relatives in a way bare bones cannot.

Susan Lemke, Math and Science Program Manager at the Fremont Unified School District in Fremont, California, gave me a science-teacher's-eye view of the concepts and language and helped make this a better, more accessible book.

I'd like to thank Tyrone Hayes and George Schaller, both extraordinary scientists, for permission to use quotations. Epidemiologist Lynne Gaffikin provided many astute comments, as did Stanford University School of Medicine professor Paul Blumenthal, who reviewed the sections on childbirth. Archeologist and expert flintknapper Allen Denover did his best to teach me how to make a stone spearpoint, although what I actually learned is that I wouldn't last very long in any paleo-context.

My critique partners Gennifer Choldenko, Diane Fraser, Marissa Moss, Elizabeth Partridge, and Emily Polsby read every word, reining me in and spurring me along with kindness and patience. Elizabeth Shreeve generously shared resources and tips as we both wrestled with writing about human evolution for young people. To my long-term writer buddies Keely Parrack and Deborah Underwood: I could not have survived the COVID lockdown without you.

Finding just the right photograph isn't easy. I am indebted to the following people and institutions for providing images and permissions: Maxime Aubert, Tony Berlant, Jennifer Clark, Andy Comins, David Coulson, Melisa Durkee, Brett Eloff, Kenneth Garrett, Melanie Norton Hugow, Sandra Jacob, Josephine Joordens, Eunice Mbindyo, David Morris, Jed Morse, Alistair Pike, Karen Lee Thompson, Tobias Wulf, the Human Origins Program at the Smithsonian Institution, the Max Planck Institute for Evolutionary Anthropology, the McGregor Museum, Museum Ulm, the Nasher Sculpture Center, the Trust for African Rock Art, and the University of Cambridge.

Many thanks to Diane Earley for so skillfully pulling together text, maps, art, and photographs to make this book a visual pleasure. I'm grateful to copyeditor Jackie Dever for her painstaking review of every dash and dot, and to Mercedes Acosta for her thoughtful comments and particular attention to areas of cultural sensitivity. I greatly appreciate the contribution of Edith Campbell, Associate Education Librarian at Indiana State University, who provided a perceptive cultural critique.

I'm deeply grateful to editor Alyssa Mito Pusey for her kind guidance and commitment to quality nonfiction for young readers. Remarkably, after enduring the source notes and bibliography of *Samurai Rising*, she was willing to work with me again on a project requiring even more documentation. For that Alyssa deserves a great deal of credit—and perhaps a vacation.

Much love to my family: Rob, Travis, Kelsey, Connor, Whitney, Jason, and Shepherd. You are the best hominins of all.

SOURCES

For bibliographic information, please see pages 153–162.

INTRODUCTION
Dolphin vs human EQ (encephalization quotients): Marino.

Characteristics of ancestral primates: Holstein and Foley; Fleagle, pp. 11–40.

30–50 copying errors in average human genome: Conrad et al.

Bacteria and virus generation times: Drexler, p. 5.

STEP 1: WE STAND UP
Number of mammal species: Burgin et al.

Uplift of Africa's rift valleys: Dartnell, pp. 11–13; Unger, pp. 72, 97.

Split between eastern and western forest apes: Suddendorf, pp. 239–241.

Adaptation of herbivores to grasslands: Potts and Sloan, p. 44.

Saber-toothed cats: Bonis et al.; Peigne et al.

Chimpanzee diets: Stanford, *New Chimpanzee*, p. 25.

Chimpanzees possessing forest-ape qualities: Tomasello, p. 14.

African Miocene fauna: Vignaud et al.

Extractive foraging: Laland, p. 109; Tomasello, p. 2.

Group living: Tomasello, pp. 14, 20–21, 31; E. O. Wilson, p. 14; and Diamond, *Third Chimpanzee*, p. 70.

Ancient apes with upright stance: Bohme et al. and Ward et al.

Advantages of upright standing and walking: Holstein and Foley, p. 13; Suddendorf, p. 242.

Sahelanthropus tchadensis and local ecology: Brunet et al. and Vignaud et al.

Orrorin tugenensis: Senut et al.

Ardipithecus kadabba: Haile-Selassie.

Adaptations for upright walking: Smith, p. 112.

Canine teeth: Gamble et al., p. 93.

Ardipithecus ramidus: Tim White et al.

Back problems in humans: Lents, p. 23.

Species of Australopith and where found: Fleagle, pp. 512–523.

Australopithecus spp. as human ancestor: Tim White et al.

Pliocene fauna: Schaller, *Golden Shadows*, pp. 256, 259.

Australopithecus afarensis (Lucy): Fleagle, pp. 513–518; Stanford, *New Chimpanzee*, pp. 193–194.

Australopith footprints: Raichlen et al.; Potts and Sloan, p. 70.

Australopith brain size: Holstein and Foley, p. 6.

Modern human brain size: Beals et al.

Australopith communication: Fleagle, p. 524; Pinker, p. 363; Stanford, *New Chimpanzee*, p. 38; Suddendorf, p. 260.

Taung Child: Gilbert et al.

Predation dangers: Schultz et al.

Chimpanzee social life, mating habits: Stanford, *Apes*, pp. 13, 27.

Australopith social life: Wynn et al., "Ape's View."

Makapansgat Pebble: Bednarik, "'Australopithecine' Cobble."

STEP 2: WE SMASH ROCKS

Chimpanzee honey-gathering: Wilifried and Yamagiwa; Stanford, *New Chimpanzee*, p. 163.

New Caledonian crow manufacture of stepped tool: Holzhaider et al.

Chimpanzee use of hammer-and-anvil tool: Stanford, *New Chimpanzee*, p. 159.

New Caledonian crow manufacture of hooked tool: Hunt.

Chimpanzee hunting of bush babies: Stanford, *New Chimpanzee*, p. 138.

Using tools to make tools unique to hominins: Holstein and Foley, p. 14.

Earliest evidence of cut marks on bones: McPherron et al.

Earliest evidence of tool manufacture: Harmand et al.

George Schaller's test of hominin survival: Schaller, *Golden Shadows*, pp. 266–269.

"And with the same tool I bashed in the back of the skull, exposing the brain, potentially a nice snack": Schaller, *Golden Shadows*, p. 269.

First stone knapping: Stanford, *New Chimpanzee*, p. 199; Sanz et al., pp. 225–240.

Advantages of edged stone tools: Zink and Lieberman; Wrangham, *Catching Fire*, p. 46.

Homo habilis description: Potts and Sloan, p. 41; Holstein and Foley, p. 7.

Tool use by male and female chimpanzees: Stanford, *New Chimpanzee*, p. 165.

Oldowan tools: Stanford, *New Chimpanzee*, p. 199; Potts and Sloan, pp. 87–89.

Homo habilis scavenging and hunting: Potts and Sloan, pp. 84–85; Suddendorf, p. 247.

"Robust" Australopiths (*Paranthropus*): Potts and Sloan, pp. 39–40.

Predation on *Paranthropus*: Potts and Sloan, p. 55.

Paranthropus use of bone tools: Stanford, *New Chimpanzee*, p. 200.

Homo habilis brain size: Holstein and Foley, p. 8.

Cognitive demands of stone knapping: Sanz et al., pp. 225–240.

Social intelligence: Laland, pp. 135–139.

Use of a home base: Fleagle, p. 532.

Chimpanzee hunting strategies: Stanford, *New Chimpanzee*, pp. 101, 130–153.

Diets of modern hunter-gatherers: Wrangham, *Catching Fire*, pp. 133–136; Noss and Hewlett.

Predation on *Homo habilis*: Potts and Sloan, pp. 47, 55.

Cooperative defense against predators: Suddendorf, p. 247.

Cooperative systems and cheating: Suddendorf, pp. 163–164.

Communication in early human ancestors: Sterelny, "Language, Gesture, Skill."

Evolution of the sclera: Kobayashi and Kohshima; Tomasello, p. 77.

STEP 3: WE GET SWELLED HEADS

Energy demands of the brain: Herculano-Houzel, p. 17; Laland, p. 235.

Climate swings and human evolution: Maslin, pp. 138–139; Dartnell, p. 22; Potts and Sloan, pp. 48, 109; deMenocal.

Homo erectus description: Holstein and Foley, pp. 8–9; Fleagle, pp. 534–535; Bastir et al.

Date of earliest *Homo erectus*: Herries et al.

Hominin brain sizes: Holstein and Foley, p. 8.

Energy expenditures, Australopith vs. Erectus: Schultz et al.

Homo erectus range and energy expenditures: Potts and Sloan, p. 67; Wrangham, *Catching Fire*, p. 5; Herculano-Houzel, p. 190.

African hunting dog predatory techniques: Schaller, *Serengeti Lion*, p. 379.

Cognitive demands of tracking and hunting: Sterelny, *Evolved Apprentice*, pp. 11–12.

Hominin adaptations for heat dissipation: Suddendorf, p. 250.

Change in skin color: Stanford, *New Chimpanzee*, p. 182.

Nariokotome Boy: Gamble et al., pp. 139, 141; Potts and Sloan, pp. 78–79; Fleagle, p. 534; Gurche, pp. 148–149.

Chimpanzee social structure: Stanford, *New Chimpanzee*, p. 29; Stanford, *Apes*, pp. 13, 27.

Bonobo social structure: Stanford, *New Chimpanzee*, p. 73; Maslin, p. 173.

Hunter-gatherer societies: E. O. Wilson, p. 21; Wrangham, *Catching Fire*, p. 136; Noss and Hewlett; Ember.

Nutritional demands of pregnancy/lactation: Martin Jones, p. 62.

Acheulean handaxes: Gamble et al., p. 119; Potts and Sloan, pp. 86, 89; Berlant and Wynn, p. 73; Wynn and Gowlett, "Handaxe Reconsidered"; Stout.

Chimpanzee/gorilla competition: Stanford, *Apes*, pp. 74, 94–5.

Hominin coexistence/competition: Stanford, *Apes*, pp. 98–99, 104; Sugden et al.; Herries et al.

Archaic hominin interbreeding with modern humans: Reich, pp. 40, 208–209.

Polar bear/grizzly bear hybrids: Pongracz et al.

Movement of hominins out of Africa: Maslin, pp. 147–148; Potts and Sloan, p. 97; Lee, p. 260.

STEP 4: WE TAKE A HIKE

Japanese writing system: Association for Japanese-Language Teaching, pp. 11–12.

Standard number of Chinese characters in Japanese (kanji): Heisig, p. 4.

Japanese as world's most complex writing system: Backhouse, p. 38.

Number of species in the Serengeti: Spawls et al., *Reptiles and Amphibians*, p. 4; Spawls et al., *Field Guide*, p. 5; Kennedy, p. 9; Foley et al., p. 8.

Environmental knowledge: Lee, p. 176; Robert Boyd, pp. 139–140; Pinker, p. 439.

Homo erectus in Dmanisi, Georgia: Holstein and Foley, p. 9.

Homo erectus in China: Ao et al.; Pu et al.

Homo erectus in Indonesia: Tyler and Sartono.

Tools found in China: Zhu et al.

Mystery hominins leaving Africa: Potts and Sloan, p. 97.

Homo floresiensis: Sutikna et al.

Homo luzonensis: Detroit et al.

Evolution of "Hobbits": Gurche, p. 268.

Asian fauna: Turner, pp. 48, 74, 81; Louys et al.

Gigantopithecus blacki: Zhao and Zhang; Welker et al.

Bamboo tools: Holstein and Foley, p. 15.

Engraved mussel shell and shell tools: Joordens et al.

Teaching: Laland, pp. 158, 319.

Teaching among nonhuman animals: Cato and Hauser; Lopez and Lopez.

Lack of teaching among bottlenose dolphins: Janet Mann, Shark Bay Dolphin Project, private communication with author.

Lack of teaching among New Caledonian crows: Gavin Hunt, University of Auckland, private communication with author.

Link between teaching and communication: Laland, pp. 29, 173; Sterelny, *Evolved Apprentice*, p. 151.

Significance of pointing: Tomasello, pp. 5, 49; Laland, p. 187; Corballis, pp. 134–135; Sterelny, *Evolved Apprentice*, p. 173.

Communication skills increasing evolutionary fitness: Laland, pp. 186–187.

Homo erectus communication skills: Gamble et al., pp. 141–142.

Theory of mind: Suddendorf, p. 114; Robert Boyd, p. 176; Corballis, p. 81.

Raven deception: Marzluff and Angell, p. 46.

Chimpanzee deception: Corballis, pp. 88–89.

Chimpanzee "adoptions": Stanford, *New Chimpanzee*, p. 122.

Homo erectus (Dmanisi, Georgia): http://www.dmanisi.ge/ website.

Toothless *Homo erectus* (Dmanisi, Georgia): Gurche, p. 182.

STEP 5: WE INVENT BARBECUE

Lightning, brushfires, foraging in rubble: Gamble et al., p. 132; Sterelny, *Evolved Apprentice*, p. 17; Fletcher, p. 174.

Advantages of cooking: Wrangham, *Catching Fire*, pp. 38, 40, 44; Wrangham, "Control of Fire"; Martin Jones, pp. 82–83, 93; Suddendorf, p. 251.

Fire and temperature regulation: Schultz et al.; Wrangham, *Catching Fire*, p.183.

Food preservation: Wrangham, "Control of Fire"; Wrangham, *Catching Fire*, p. 194.

Tool hardening: Gamble et al., p. 118.

Protection from predators: Wrangham, *Catching Fire*, p. 99.

Pleistocene predators: Turner, pp. 41–44, 48, 84, 203.

Fire and social life: Wrangham, *Catching Fire*, p. 153; Dunbar, p. 195; E. O. Wilson, p. 22.

Ancient evidence of fire: Dunbar, pp. 163–165.

Cultural evolution: Tomasello, p. 83.

The cooking hypothesis: Wrangham, "Control of Fire."

Alternatives to the cooking hypothesis: Aiello and Wheeler.

Genetic adaptation to smoke (AHR protein): Hubbard et al.

Fire-starting with rocks and flint: Wrangham, *Catching Fire*, pp. 191–192.

Transmission of innovation: Sterelny, *Evolved Apprentice*, pp. 13, 59–61; Potts and Sloan, p. 125.

Homo heidelbergensis: Maslin, pp. 37–38; Potts and Sloan, p. 98; Fleagle, p. 535; Holstein and Foley, p. 8.

Hominin vs dolphin EQ (encephalization quotient): Marino.

European Pleistocene fauna: Matze, Gaudzinski et al.; Reumer et al.; Camarós et al.

STEP 6: WE START TALKING (AND NEVER SHUT UP)

Chimpanzee and bonobo language abilities: Pinker, pp. 348–350; Suddendorf, pp. 83, 85–86.

Human production of words and grammar: Pinker, pp. 9, 379; Sterelny, "Language, Gesture, Skill."

Great ape and toddler gestures: Kersken et al.

Human vocabularies: Pinker, p. 145.

Language aids teaching and learning: Laland, pp. 29, 173, 183, 185–188.

Language and planning/cooperation: Potts and Sloan, p. 164; Tomasello, p. 5; Suddendorf, pp. 78, 90, 96; Sterelny, "Language, Gesture, Skill."

Language as verbal grooming: Dunbar, p. 227; Sterelny, "Language, Gesture, Skill"; Lee, p. 174.

Gossip and the craving for social information: E. O. Wilson, p. 190; Dunbar, pp. 263, 269; Brian Boyd, "On the Origin," pp. 64, 165; Laland, p. 176.

Homo heidelbergensis and language: Gamble et al., pp. 32, 141; Dunbar, p. 238; Gurche, p. 194.

Language and toolmaking: Corballis, pp. 184–186; Stout and Khreisheh; Morgan et al.; Kolodny and Edelman.

Advantages and disadvantages of slow growth: Schultz et al.; Dunbar, p. 64.

Hominin childbirth: Maslin, pp. 160–162; Potts and Sloan, p. 74; Dunbar, p. 245; Lee, p. 60.

Helplessness of human babies: Gurche, p. 150; Martin Jones, p. 87; Dunbar, p. 245.

Importance of social group for child-raising: Maslin, pp. 160–162.

Homo heidelbergensis descendants: Dunbar, p. 183; Maslin, p. 38; Holstein and Foley, p. 9.

Homo neanderthalensis description and selection pressures: Maslin, p. 37; Gurche, pp. 219, 221; Potts and Sloan, p. 99.

Homo neanderthalensis and *Homo sapiens* brain sizes: Ruff et al.; Martin Jones, p. 82; Beals et al.

FOXP2: Reich, p. 8; Potts and Sloan, p. 131; Fitch, p. 168.

Homo neanderthalensis language capability: Gurche, p. 229; Gamble et al., p. 142; Sejnowski, p. 140; Dunbar, p. 244; Barney et al.; Martinez et al., "Human Hyoid Bones"; Conde-Valverde et al.

Homo neanderthalensis auditory capacities: Martinez et al., "Auditory Capacities."

First known lethal violence: Sala et al.

Homo neanderthalensis spears: Although the original paper announcing the discovery of the spears calculated an age of 400,000 years, additional analysis reports an age of 300,000 years. Schoch et al.

Language as a cultural standard: Corballis, p. 194.

Language and composite tools: Suddendorf, p. 257.

Homo neanderthalensis technology: Sterelny, *Evolved Apprentice*, p. 13; Gurche, p. 225; Fleagle, p. 537; Maslin, p. 179; Smith, p. 201; Berlant and Wynn, pp. 150–151; Hardy et al.

Homo neanderthalensis exploitation of seafood: Villa et al.; Trinkaus et al.; Zilhao et al.

Homo neanderthalensis care of disabled: Potts and Sloan, p. 52; Gracia et al.

Homo neanderthalensis footprints: Duveau et al.

Homo neanderthalensis cannibalism: Gurche, p. 232; Suddendorf, p. 266.

Homo neanderthalensis burials: Gurche, p. 231; Gamble et al., p. 172.

Homo neanderthalensis stalagmite constructions: Jaubert et al.

STEP 7: WE BECOME STORYTELLERS

Origins of *Homo sapiens*: Maslin, p. 170; Gurche, p. 300; Brooks et al.; Potts et al.

Homo sapiens fossil from North Africa: Hublin et al., "New Fossil."

Homo sapiens fossil from South Africa: Stringer.

Early *Homo sapiens* in East Africa: Maslin, p. 38; Holstein and Foley, p. 11; Suddendorf, p. 234; Nielsen et al.

Early *Homo sapiens* in Greece and Israel: Harvati et al.; Hershkovitz et al.

Evidence of early mixing of *Homo sapiens* and *Homo neanderthalensis*: Price et al.; Petr et al.

Markers of symbolic thought: Gamble et al., p. 138; Potts and Sloan, pp. 119, 164; Pagel, p. 278.

!Xoo and Tuyaca: *The Economist*; Pereltsvaig, pp. 202–205.

Universality of language: Pinker, p. 364.

Inverse relationship between cultural complexity and language complexity: Corballis, p. 17.

Advantage of symbolic communication: Corballis, p. 172; Suddendorf, p. 250.

Chimpanzee and bonobo understanding of symbols: Potts and Sloan, p. 129.

Jewelry as symbolic communication: Sterelny, *Evolved Apprentice*, pp. 50–51; Potts and Sloan, p. 137.

Ancient African beads: Potts and Sloan, p. 119; Vanhaeren et al.

Ancient African ochre: Gamble et al., p. 171; Henshilwood et al., "Emergence of Modern"; Henshilwood et al., "A 100,000-Year-Old"; Sterelny, *Evolved Apprentice*, p. 53.

Homo neanderthalensis jewelry: Radovčić et al.; Hoffman et al., "Symbolic Use."

Homo neanderthalensis cave paintings: Although Hoffman et al. have dated these paintings to at least 64,000 years ago ("U-Th Dating"), this date has been challenged by other researchers (Randall White et al.). Hoffman et al. stand by their original analysis.

Homo sapiens population bottleneck and near-extinction: Reich, p. 241; Maslin, p. 181; Holstein and Foley, p. 11; Dartnell, p. 46.

Homo sapiens refugia during climate stress: Marean et al.; Chan et al.

Second *Homo sapiens* migration out of Africa: Holstein and Foley, p. 12; Dunbar, pp. 217, 220; Dartnell, pp. 46–47; Gurche, p. 228. Although many scientists date this migration to sometime after 100,000 years ago, recent evidence (120,000-year-old footprints in Saudi Arabia and human teeth found in China that may date to as early as 120,000 years ago) suggests an earlier exit. See Stewart et al.; Wu et al.

Homo sapiens and environment in the Middle East: Groucutt et al.

Hominin species circa 100,000 years ago: Dartnell, p. 47; Reich, p. 64.

Appearance of Denisovans: Gokhman et al.

Homo erectus and Denisovan possible hybridization: Nielsen et al.; Rodgers et al.

Homo erectus in Java: Although these were originally dated to as recent as 26,000 years ago, new analysis dates the Java fossils to no later than 110,000 years ago. See Rizal et al.

Homo floresiensis: Sutikna et al.

Homo luzonensis: Detroit et al.

Homo neanderthalensis appearance: Suddendorf, p. 258.

Homo sapiens and *Homo neanderthalensis* hybridization: Reich, pp. 40–42; Pääbo, pp. 190–199; Smith, p. 201.

Dental bacteria of *Homo sapiens* and *Homo neanderthalensis*: Weyrich et al.

Homo neanderthalensis and Denisovan hybridization: Slon et al., 2018.

Homo sapiens and Denisovan hybridization: Pääbo, pp. 246–247.

African *Homo sapiens* and Neanderthal ancestry: Chen et al.; Price et al.

African *Homo sapiens* and archaic genomes: Reich, p. 209; Lachance et al.; Durvasula and Sankararaman.

Deep history of population mixing: Reich, p. 231.

Evolutionary advantages of hybridization with *Homo neanderthalensis* and Denisovans: Abi-Rached et al.; Enard and Petrov; Huerta-Sanchez et al.

Homo sapiens migration to Southeast Asia: Smith, p. 179; Suddendorf, pp. 234–235.

Homo floresiensis and Flores fauna: Sutikna et al.

Dispersal of elephants by swimming: Quammen, *Song of the Dodo*, pp. 153–157.

Island gigantism/island dwarfism: Diamond, "Did Komodo Dragons Evolve?"; Quammen, *Song of the Dodo*, pp. 157–158.

Komodo dragon presence on Flores: *Jakarta Post.*

Homo sapiens migration to Australia: Clarkson et al.

Australian fauna during the Pleistocene: Kaars et al.; MacPhee, pp. 94–95, 122–123.

Middle/late Stone Age technology: Potts and Sloan, pp. 120–121; Laland, p. 10; Lombard and Phillipson.

Homo sapiens arrival in Europe: Hublin et al., "Initial Upper Palaeolithic," Prüfer et al.; Gibbons.

Survival challenges of Ice Age Europe: Dunbar, p. 182; Sterelny, *Evolved Apprentice*, pp. 62–64, 68; Dartnell, p. 33.

Homo sapiens social networks and their advantages: Potts and Sloan, pp. 120–121, 125, 164; Gurche, p. 302; Dunbar, p. 251; Robert Boyd, pp. 20, 34.

Uses of narrative: Gottscall, pp. 87, 148, 187, 189–190; Brian Boyd, "Jane, Meet Charles," pp. 10–11; Brian Boyd, "On the Origin," pp. 64, 104, 162–168, 19; Sterelny, *Evolved Apprentice*, p. 163; Suddendorf, pp. 216, 221–222.

Narrative as coping mechanisms: Corballis, pp. 104–105.

Theory of mind and the supernatural: Corballis, pp. 112–113; Dunbar, p. 234.

Supernatural beings as rule-breakers: Boyer, p. 78.

Dating of Budj Bim volcano: Matchan et al.

Dating of Sulawesi cave paintings: Aubert et al., "Earliest Hunting Scene."

Dating of Chauvet Cave: Cuzange et al.

Dating of Lion Man statue: Kind et al.

Dating of Lascaux Cave: Although the standard date of the Lascaux paintings is usually given as 17,000 years ago, this rests on shaky evidence (see Bahn). The date of 16,000 years for the famous "shaft scene" is based on carbon-14 dating of charcoal found in the shaft.

Conclusion: We Dominate

Homo floresiensis: Sutikna et al.

Homo luzonensis: Detroit et al.

Homo erectus in Java: Although they were originally dated to as recent as 26,000 years ago, new analysis dates the Java fossils to no later than 110,000 years ago. See Rizal et al.

Homo erectus extinction due to climate change: Raia et al.

Homo neanderthalensis extinction: Sterelny, *The Evolved Apprentice,* pp. 62–64, 68; Dunbar, p. 250; Gurche, p. 226, 233; Reich, p. 90; Potts and Sloan, p. 145; Diamond, *Third Chimpanzee*, p. 54; Kolodny and Feldman; Raia et al.

Most recent Denisovan fossils: Douka et al., Ji et al.

Late hybridization between *Homo sapiens* and Denisovans: Jacobs et al.; GenomeAsia 100K Consortium.

Human migration to the Americas: Ardelean et al.

American fauna at the time of human migration: Mithen, pp. 236–245.

Warming of climate and retreat of ice sheets: Potts and Sloan, p. 152.

Date of first agriculture: Diamond, *World Until Yesterday*, p. 6.

Date of first cities: Wengrow, p. xiii.

Date of first writing: Diamond, *World Until Yesterday*, p. 6; Dong, p. 2.

Date of first emoji poetry: Stephanie Berger, private communication.

Conversion of natural ecosystems: Goldewijk et al.

Biomass of wild vs. domestic birds, wild mammals vs. humans, and domestic mammals: Bar-On et al.

Decline of wildlife populations, recovery of diversity: World Wildlife Fund; Davis et al.

Threats to oceans: Kendall Jones et al.

Threat of climate change: Intergovernmental Panel on Climate Change.

Human cooperation: Tomasello, p. 82; Robert Boyd, p. 160.

Sulawesi hand stencil: Aubert et al., "Pleistocene Cave Art"; the hand stencils in this image were not datable, but are similar to nearby stencils dated to at least 40,000 years old. Maxime Aubert, email message to author, July 15, 2020.

Spanish hand stencil: Pike et al.

Australian hand stencil: Undated, from Buckland Tableland, Central Queensland Highlands, Australia.

African hand stencil: Undated, from Wadi el Obeiyed, Egypt.

South American hand stencil: Cueva de las Manos (Cave of the Hands), Argentina. The hand stencils at Cueva de las Manos, a UNESCO World Heritage site, have been dated to 13,000 to 9,500 years ago. UNESCO.

A Note on Race
Race and genetics: American Association of Physical Anthropologists.

Lactose tolerance: Reich, pp. 223–225; Itan et al.

Sickle cell disease: Foy et al.; Reich, pp. 223–225.

Tyrone Hayes quote (used with Dr. Hayes's permission): Hayes.

More on Evolution
Sex selection: Coyne, pp. 144–167.

Genetic drift: Quammen, *Song of the Dodo*, pp. 517–518; Coyne, pp. 123–124.

Horizontal gene transfer: Quammen, *Tangled Tree*.

De novo evolution: Levy.

Charles Darwin quote: Darwin, p. 513.

More About Dating Fossils, Artifacts, and Climate Shifts
Dating technologies: Potts and Sloan, p. 41.

Carbon-14: Reich, p. 274.

Calcite dating: Aubert et al., "Pleistocene Cave Art."

Molecular clocks: Pääbo, p. 66.

Proteomics and *Gigantopithecus blacki*: Welker et al.

Dating of climate shifts: Potts and Sloan, p. 50.

BIBLIOGRAPHY

Abi-Rached, Laurent, et al. "The Shaping of Modern Human Immune Systems by Multiregional Admixture with Archaic Humans." *Science* 334, no. 6052 (2011): 89–94.

Aiello, Leslie C., and Peter Wheeler. "The Expensive-Tissue Hypothesis." *Current Anthropology* 36, no. 2 (1995): 191–221.

American Association of Physical Anthropologists. "AAPA Statement on Race and Racism." https://physanth.org/about/position-statements/aapa-statement-race-and-racism-2019/

Ao, Hong, et al. "New Evidence for Early Presence of Hominids in North China." *Scientific Reports* 3, no. 2403 (2013). doi:10.1038/srep02403

Ardelean, Ciprian F., et al. "Evidence of Human Occupation in Mexico Around the Last Glacial Maximum." *Nature* 584 (2020): 87–92. doi:10.1038/s41586-020-2509-0

Association for Japanese-Language Teaching. *Japanese for Busy People I.* Tokyo, Japan: Kodansha International, 1984.

Aubert, M., et al. "Earliest Hunting Scene in Prehistoric Art." *Nature* 576 (2019): 442–445. doi:10.1038/s41586-019-1806-y

Aubert, M., et al. "Pleistocene Cave Art from Sulawesi, Indonesia." *Nature* 514 (2014): 223–227.

Backhouse, A. E. *The Japanese Language: An Introduction.* Oxford, UK: Oxford University Press, 1993.

Bahn, Paul G. "The Impact of Direct Dating of Palaeolithic Cave Art: Lascaux Revisited." *Anthropologie* 33, no. 3 (1995): 191–199.

Barney, Ann, et al. "Articulatory Capacity of Neanderthals, a Very Recent and Human-Like Fossil Hominin." *Philosophical Transactions of the Royal Society B* 167 (2012), 88–102.

Bar-On, Yinon M. "The Biomass Distribution on Earth." *Proceedings of the Royal Academy of Sciences* 115, no. 25 (2018): 6506–6511.

Bastir, Markus, et al. "Rib Cage Anatomy in *Homo erectus* Suggests a Recent Evolutionary Origin of Modern Human Body Shape." *Nature Ecology & Evolution* 4 (2020): 1178–1187. doi:10.1038/s41559-020-1240-4

Beals, Kenneth L., et al. "Brain Size, Cranial Morphology, Climate, and Time Machines." *Current Anthropology* 25, no. 333 (1984): 301–330.

Bednarik, Robert G. "The 'Australopithecine' Cobble from Makapansgat, South Africa." *South African Archeological Bulletin* 53 (1998): 4–8.

Berlant, Tony, and Thomas Wynn. *First Sculpture: Handaxe to Figure Stone.* Dallas, TX: Nasher Sculpture Center, 2018.

Bohme, Madelaine, et al. "A New Miocene Ape and Locomotion in the Ancestor of Great Apes and Humans." *Nature* 575 (2019): 489–493.

Bonis, Louis de, et al. "New Sabre-Toothed Cats in the Late Miocene of Toros Menalla (Chad)." *Comptes Rendus Palevol* 9, no. 5 (2010): 221–227.

Boyd, Brian. "Jane, Meet Charles: Literature, Evolution, and Human Nature." *Philosophy and Literature* 22, no. 1 (1998): 1–30.

Boyd, Brian. *On the Origin of Stories: Evolution, Cognition, and Fiction.* Cambridge, MA: Belknap Press of Harvard University Press, 2009.

Boyd, Robert. *A Different Kind of Animal: How Culture Transformed Our Species.* Princeton, NJ: Princeton University Press, 2018.

Boyer, Pascal. *Religion Explained*. New York: Basic Books, 2001.

Brooks, Alison S., et al. "Long-Distance Stone Transport and Pigment Use in the Earliest Middle Stone Age." *Science* 360, no. 6384 (2018): 90–94.

Brunet, M., et al. "A New Hominin from the Upper Miocene of Chad, Central Africa." *Nature* 418, no. 6894 (2002): 145–151.

Burgin, Connor J., et al. "How Many Species of Mammals Are There?" *Journal of Mammalogy* 99, no. 1 (2018): 1–14.

Camarós, Edgard, et al. "The Evolution of Paleolithic Hominin-Carnivore Interaction Written in Teeth: Stories from the Swabian Jura (Germany). *Journal of Archeological Science: Reports* 6 (2016): 798–809.

Cato, T. M., and M. D. Hauser. "Is There Teaching in Nonhuman Animals?" *The Quarterly Review of Biology* 67, no. 2 (1992): 151–174.

Chan, Eva K. F., et al. "Human Origins in a Southern African Paleo-Wetland and First Migrations." *Nature* 575 (2019): 185–189.

Chen, Lu, et al. "Identifying and Interpreting Apparent Neanderthal Ancestry in African Individuals." *Cell* 180, no. 4 (2020): 677–687.

Clarkson, Chris, et al. "Human Occupation of Northern Australia by 65,000 Years Ago." *Nature* 547 (2017): 306–310.

Conde-Valverde, Mercedes, et al. "Neanderthals and *Homo sapiens* Had Similar Auditory and Speech Capacities." *Nature Ecology and Evolution* (2021). doi:10.1038/s41559-021-01391-6

Conrad, D., et al. "Variation in Genome-Wide Mutation Rates Within and Between Human Families." *Nature Genetics* 43 (2011): 712–714.

Corballis, Michael C. *The Truth About Language: What It Is and Where It Came From*. Chicago: University of Chicago Press, 2017.

Coyne, Jerry A. *Why Evolution Is True*. New York: Viking, 2010.

Cuzange, Marie-Therese, et al. "Radiocarbon Intercomparison Program for Chauvet Cave." *Radiocarbon* 49, no. 2 (2007): 339–347.

Dartnell, Lewis. *Origins: How the Earth Made Us*. London: Penguin Random House UK, 2018.

Darwin, Charles. *On the Origin of Species*. New York: Sterling, 2008. Based on first edition published 1859 by John Murray, London.

Davis, Matt, et al. "Mammal Diversity Will Take Millions of Years to Recover from the Current Biodiversity Crisis." *Proceedings of the National Academy of Science* 115, no. 44 (2018): 11262–11267.

deMenocal, Peter B. "Climate and Human Evolution." *Science* 331, no. 6017 (2011): 540–542.

Detroit, Florent, et al. "A New Species of *Homo* from the Late Pleistocene of the Philippines." *Nature* 568 (2019): 181–186.

Diamond, Jared. "Did Komodo Dragons Evolve to Eat Pygmy Elephants?" *Nature* 326 (1987): 832.

Diamond, Jared. *The Third Chimpanzee: The Evolution and Future of the Human Animal*. New York: HarperCollins, 1992.

Diamond, Jared. *The World Until Yesterday: What Can We Learn from Traditional Societies?* New York: Viking, 2012.

Dong, Hongyuan. *A History of the Chinese Language*. London: Routledge, 2014.

Douka, Katerina, et al. "Age Estimate for Hominin Fossils and the Onset of the Upper Palaeolithic at Denisova Cave." *Nature* 565 (2019): 640–644.

Drexler, M. *What You Need to Know About Infectious Disease*. Washington, DC: National Academies Press, 2010.

Dunbar, Robin. *Human Evolution: Our Brains and Behavior*. Oxford, UK: Oxford University Press, 2016.

Durvasula, Arun, and Sriram Sankararaman. "Recovering Signals of Ghost Archaic Introgression in African Populations." *Science Advances* 6, no. 7 (2020): eaax5097. doi:10.1126/sciadv.aax5097

Duveau, Jeremy, et al. "The Composition of a Neandertal Social Group Revealed by Hominin Footprints at Le Rozel (Normandy, France)." *Proceedings of the National Academy of Sciences* 116, no. 39 (2019): 19409–19414.

Economist, The. "Tongue Twisters: In Search of the World's Hardest Language." December 17, 2009.

Ember, Carol. "Residential Variation Among Hunter-Gatherers." *Behavior Science Research* 10, no. 3 (1975): 199–227.

Enard, David, and Dmitri Petrov. "Evidence that RNA Viruses Drove Adaptive Introgression Between Neanderthals and Modern Humans." *Cell* 175, no. 2 (2018): 360–371.

Fitch, Tecumseh. "More Than Just Small Talk." In *Sydney Brenner's 10-on-10: The Chronicles of Evolution*, edited by Sydney Brenner, 161–169. Singapore: Wildtype Books, 2019.

Fleagle, John G. *Primate Adaptation and Evolution*. 2nd ed. San Diego: Academic Press, 1999.

Fletcher, Roland. "The Logic of Cultural Evolution." In *Sydney Brenner's 10-on-10: The Chronicles of Evolution*, edited by Sydney Brenner, 171–179. Singapore: Wildtype Books, 2019.

Foley, Charles, et al. *A Field Guide to the Larger Mammals of Tanzania*. Princeton, NJ: Princeton University Press, 2014.

Foy, Henry, et al. "The Variability of Sickle-Cell Rates in the Tribes of Kenya and the Southern Sudan." *The British Medical Journal* 1, no. 4857 (1954): 294–297.

Gamble, Clive, et al. *Thinking Big: How the Evolution of Social Life Shaped the Human Mind*. New York: Thames and Hudson, 2014.

Gaudzinski, Sabine, et al. "Paleoecology and Archaeology of the Karlich-Seeufer Open-Air Site (Middle Pleistocene) in the Central Rhineland, Germany." *Quaternary Research* 46, no. 3 (1996): 319–334.

GenomeAsia 100K Consortium. "The GenomeAsia 100K Project Enables Genetic Discoveries Across Asia." *Nature* 576 (2019): 106–111.

Gibbons, Ann. "More Than 45,000 Years Ago, Modern Humans Ventured into Neanderthal Territory. Here's What Happened Next." *Science* (2021): doi:10.1126/science.abi8830.

Gilbert, C. C., et al. "Brief Communication: Plio-Pleistocene Eagle Predation on Fossil Cercopithecids from the Humpata Plateau, Southern Angola." *American Journal of Physical Anthropology* 139, no. 3 (2009): 421–429.

Gokhman, David, et al. "Reconstructing Denisovan Anatomy Using DNA Methylation Maps." *Cell* 179, no. 1 (2019): 180–192.

Goldewijk, Kees Klein, et al. "The HYDE 3.1 Spatially Explicit Database of Human-Induced Global Land-Use Change over the Past 12,000 Years." *Global Ecology and Biogeography* 20, no. 1 (2011): 73–86.

Gottscall, Jonathan, ed. *The Literary Animal: Evolution and the Nature of Narrative*. Evanston, IL: Northwestern University Press, 2005.

Gracia, Ana, et al. "Craniosynostosis in the Middle Pleistocene Human Cranium 14 from the Sima de los Huesos, Atapuerca, Spain." *Proceedings of the National Academy of Sciences* 106, no. 16 (2009): 6573–6578.

Groucutt, Huw S., et al. "*Homo sapiens* in Arabia by 85,000 Years Ago." *Nature Ecology & Evolution* 2 (2018): 800–809.

Gurche, John. *Shaping Humanity: How Science, Art and Imagination Help Us Understand Our Origins.* New Haven, CT: Yale University Press, 2013.

Haile-Selassie, Y. "Late Miocene Hominids from the Middle Awash, Ethiopia." *Nature* 412 (2001): 178–181.

Hardy, B. L., et al. "Direct Evidence of Neanderthal Fibre Technology and Its Cognitive and Behavioral Implications." *Scientific Reports* 10, no. 4889 (2020). doi:10.1038/s41598-020-61839-w

Harmand, Sonia, et al. "3.3-Million-Year-Old Stone Tools from Lomekwi 3, West Turkana, Kenya." *Nature* 521 (2015): 310–315.

Harvati, Katerina, et al. "Apidima Cave Fossils Provide Earliest Evidence of *Homo sapiens* in Eurasia." *Nature* 571 (2019): 500–514.

Hayes, Tyrone. "My Dream Come True: An Open Letter to My Colleagues." Rothfels Lab. June 4, 2020. https://rothfelslab.berkeley.edu/2020/06/04/the-rothfels-lab-stands-against-racism-everywhere/

Heisig, James W. *Remembering the Kanji: A Complete Course on How Not to Forget the Meaning and Writing of Japanese Characters.* Vol. 1. Honolulu, HI: University of Hawai'i Press, 2007.

Henshilwood, Christopher S., et al. "Emergence of Modern Human Behavior: Middle Stone Age Engravings from South Africa." *Science* 295, no. 5558 (2002): 1278–1280.

Henshilwood, Christopher S., et al. "A 100,000-Year-Old Ochre-Processing Workshop at Blombos Cave, South Africa." *Science* 334, no. 6053 (2011): 219–222.

Herculano-Houzel, Suzana. *The Human Advantage: How Our Brains Became Remarkable.* Cambridge, MA: The MIT Press, 2016.

Herries, Andy I. R., et al. "Contemporaneity of *Australopithecus*, *Paranthropus*, and Early *Homo erectus* in South Africa." *Science* 368, no. 6486 (2020): eaaw7293. doi:10.1126/science.aaw7293

Hershkovitz, Israel, et al. "The Earliest Modern Humans Outside Africa." *Science* 359, no. 6374 (2018): 456–459.

Hoffman, Dirk L., et al. "Symbolic Use of Marine Shells and Mineral Pigments by Iberian Neandertals 115,000 Years Ago." *Science Advances* 4, no. 2 (2018): eaar5255. doi:10.1126/sciadv.aar5255

Hoffman, Dirk L., et al. "U-Th Dating of Carbonate Crusts Reveals Neandertal Origin of Iberian Cave Art." *Science* 359 (2018): 912–915.

Holstein, Laura van, and Robert Foley. "Hominin Evolution." In *Encyclopedia of Evolutionary Psychological Science*, edited by Todd K Shackelford and Viviana A Weekes-Shackelford. Springer International Publishing, 2017. doi:10.1007/978-3-319-16999-6_3416-1

Holzhaider, Jennifer C., et al. "The Development of Pandanus Tool Manufacture in Wild New Caledonian Crows." *Behaviour* 147, no. 5 (2010): 553–586.

Hubbard, Troy D., et al. "Divergent Ah Receptor Ligand Selectivity During Hominin Evolution." *Molecular Biology and Evolution* 33, no. 10 (2016): 2648–2658.

Hublin, Jean-Jacques, et al. "Initial Upper Palaeolithic *Homo sapiens* from Bacho Kiro Cave, Bulgaria." *Nature* 581 (2020): 299–302.

Hublin, Jean-Jacques, et al. "New Fossils from Jebel Irhoud, Morocco, and the Pan-African Origin of *Homo sapiens*." *Nature* 546 (2017): 289–292.

Huerta-Sanchez, Emilia, et al. "Altitude Adaptation in Tibetans Caused by Introgression of Denisovan-Like DNA." *Nature* 512 (2014): 194–197.

Hunt, Gavin R. "Manufacture and Use of Hook-Tools by New Caledonian Crows." *Nature* 379 (1996): 249–251.

Intergovernmental Panel on Climate Change. "Global Warming of 1.5°C: An IPCC Special Report." 2018. https://www.ipcc.ch/site/assets/uploads/sites/2/2019/06/SR15_Full_Report_Low_Res.pdf

Itan, Yuval, et al. "A Worldwide Correlation of Lactase Persistence Phenotype and Genotype." *BMC Evolutionary Biology* 10, no. 36 (2010). doi:10.1186/1471-2148-10-36

Jacobs, Guy S., et al. "Multiple Deeply Divergent Denisovan Ancestries in Papuans." *Cell* 177, no. 4 (2019): 1010–1021.

Jakarta Post. "Komodo Dragons in National Park Differ from Those on Flores Island." July 22, 2019. https://www.thejakartapost.com/travel/2019/07/20/komodo-dragons-in-national-park-differ-from-those-on-flores-island.html

Jaubert, Jacques, et al. "Early Neanderthal Constructions Deep in Bruniquel Cave in Southwestern France." *Nature* 534 (2016): 111–114.

Ji, Quang, et al. "Late Middle Pleistocene Harbin Cranium Represents a New *Homo* Species." *The Innovation* (June 25, 2021). doi:10.1015/j.xinn.2021.100132

Jones, Kendall, et al. "The Location and Protection Status of Earth's Diminishing Marine Wilderness." *Current Biology* 28, no. 15 (2018): 2506–2512e3.

Jones, Martin. *Feast: Why Humans Share Food.* Oxford, UK: Oxford University Press, 2007.

Joordens, Josephine C. A., et al. "*Homo erectus* at Trinil on Java Used Shells for Tool Production and Engraving." *Nature* 518 (2015): 228–231.

Kaars, Sander van der, et al. "Humans Rather than Climate Primary Cause of Pleistocene Megafaunal Extinction in Australia." *Nature Communications* 8, no. 14142 (2017). doi:10.1038/ncomms14142

Kennedy, Adam Scott. *Birds of the Serengeti and Ngorongoro Conservation Area.* Princeton, NJ: Princeton University Press, 2014.

Kersken, Verena, et al. "A Gestural Repertoire of 1- to 2-Year-Old Human Children: In Search of the Ape Gestures." *Animal Cognition* 22, no. 4 (2019): 577–595.

Kind, Claus-Joachim, et al. "The Smile of the Lion Man: Recent Excavations in Stadel Cave (Baden-Wurttemberg, Southwestern Germany) and the Restoration of the Famous Upper Paleolithic Figurine." *Quartar* 61 (2014): 129–145.

Kobayashi, H., and S. Kohshima. "Unique Morphology of the Human Eye and Its Adaptive Meaning: Comparative Studies on External Morphology of the Primate Eye." *Journal of Human Evolution* 40, no. 5 (2001): 419–435.

Kolodny, Oren, and Shimon Edelman. "The Evolution of the Capacity for Language: The Ecological Context and Adaptive Value of a Process of Cognitive Hijacking." *Philosophical Transactions of the Royal Society B* 373 (2018). doi:10.1098/rstb.2017.0052

Kolodny, Oren, and Marcus W. Feldman. "A Parsimonious Neutral Model Suggests Neanderthal Replacement Was Determined by Migration and Random Species Drift." *Nature Communications* 8, no. 1040 (2017). doi:10.1038/s41467-017-01043-z

Lachance, J., et al. "Evolutionary History and Adaptation from High-Coverage Whole-Genome Sequences of Diverse African Hunter-Gatherers." *Cell* 150 (2012): 457–469.

Laland, Kevin N. *Darwin's Unfinished Symphony: How Culture Made the Human Mind.* Princeton, NJ: Princeton University Press, 2017.

Lee, Sang-Hee. *Close Encounters with Humankind: A Paleoanthropologist Investigates Our Evolving Species.* New York: W. W. Norton and Company, 2018.

Lents, Nathan. *Human Errors: A Panorama of Our Glitches, from Pointless Bones to Broken Genes*. Boston: Houghton Mifflin Harcourt, 2018.

Levy, Adam. "How Evolution Builds Genes from Scratch." *Nature* 574 (2019): 314–316.

Lombard, Marlize, and Laurel Phillipson. "Indications of Bow and Stone-Tipped Arrow Use 64,000 Years Ago in KwaZulu-Natal, South Africa." *Antiquity* 84, no. 325 (2010): 635–648.

Lopez, Juan Carlos, and Diana Lopez. "Killer Whales (*Orcinus orca*) of Patagonia, and Their Behavior of Intentional Stranding While Hunting Nearshore." *Journal of Mammalogy* 66, no. 1 (1985): 181–183.

Louys, Julien, et al. "Characteristics of Pleistocene Megafauna Extinctions in Southeast Asia." *Palaeogeography, Palaeoclimatology, Palaeoecology* 243 (2007): 152–173.

Lovejoy, C. Owen, et al. "The Pelvis and Femur of *Ardipithecus ramidus*: The Emergence of Upright Walking." *Science* 326, no. 5949 (2009): 71–76.

MacPhee, Ross D. E. *End of the Megafauna*. New York: W. W. Norton and Company, 2018.

Marean, Curtis W., et al. "Early Human Use of Marine Resources and Pigment in South Africa During the Middle Pleistocene." *Nature* 449 (2007): 905–908.

Marino, Lori. "Turning the Empirical Corner on Fi : The Probability of Complex Intelligence." In *Bioastronomy '99: A New Era in Bioastronomy*, ASP Conference Series, vol. 213, edited by Guillermo A. Lemarchand and Karen J. Meech, 431–435. San Francisco, CA: Astronomical Society of the Pacific, 2000.

Martinez, I., et al. "Auditory Capacities in Middle Pleistocene Humans from the Sierra de Atapuerca in Spain." *Proceedings of the National Academy of Sciences* 101, no. 27 (2004): 9976–9981.

Martinez, I., et al. "Human Hyoid Bones from the Middle Pleistocene Site of the Sima de los Huesos (Sierra de Atapuerca, Spain)." *Journal of Human Evolution* 54, no. 1 (2008): 118–124.

Marzluff, John M., and Tony Angell. *In the Company of Crows and Ravens*. New Haven, CT: Yale University Press, 2005.

Maslin, Mark. *The Cradle of Humanity: How the Changing Landscape of Africa Made Us So Smart*. Oxford, UK: Oxford University Press, 2017.

Matchan, Erin L., et al. "Early Human Occupation of Southeastern Australia: New Insights from 40Ar/39Ar Dating of Young Volcanoes." *Geology* 48, no. 4 (2020): 390–394. doi:10.1130/G47166.1

Matze, Lobke. "The Middle Pleistocene Fauna from Schöningen (Lower Saxony, Germany): What Do the Large Mammals Tell Us?" Master's thesis, Leiden University, 2010. https://studenttheses.universiteitleiden.nl/handle/1887/18818

McPherron, Shannon P., et al. "Evidence for Stone-Tool-Assisted Consumption of Animal Tissues Before 3.39 Million Years Ago at Dikika, Ethiopia." *Nature* 466 (2010): 857–860.

Mithen, Steven. *After the Ice: A Global Human History 20,000–5,000 BC*. London: Weidenfeld and Nicolson Ltd., 2003.

Morgan, T. J. H., et al. "Experimental Evidence for the Co-Evolution of Hominin Tool-Making, Teaching, and Language." *Nature Communications* 6 (2015): 6029. doi:10.1038/ncomms7029

Nielsen, Rasmus, et al. "Tracing the Peopling of the World Through Genomics." *Nature* 541 (2017): 302–310.

Noss, Andrew, and Barry Hewlett. "The Contexts of Female Hunting in Central Africa." *American Anthropologist* 103, no. 4 (2001): 1024–1040.

Pääbo, Svante. *Neanderthal Man: In Search of Lost Genomes*. New York: Basic Books, 2014.

Pagel, Mark. *Wired for Culture: Origins of the Human Social Mind*. New York: W. W. Norton and Company, 2013.

Peigne, Stephanie, et al. "A New Machairodontine (Carnivora, Felidae) from the Late Miocene Hominid Locality of TM 266, Toros-Menalla, Chad." *Comptes Rendus Palevol* 4, no. 3 (2005): 243–253.

Pereltsvaig, Asya. *Languages of the World: An Introduction.* Cambridge, UK: Cambridge University Press, 2017.

Petr, Martin, et al. "The Evolutionary History of Neanderthal and Denisovan Y Chromosomes." *Science* 369, no. 6511 (2020): 1653–1656.

Pike, A. W. G., et al. "U-Series Dating of Paleolithic Art in 11 Caves in Spain." *Science* 336, no. 6087 (2012): 1409–1413.

Pinker, Steven. *The Language Instinct: How the Mind Creates Language.* New York: William Morrow and Company, 1994.

Pongracz, Jodie D., et al. "Recent Hybridization Between a Polar Bear and Grizzly Bears in the Canadian Arctic." *Arctic* 70, no. 2 (2017): 151–160.

Potts, Richard, and Christopher Sloan. *What Does It Mean to Be Human?* Washington, DC: National Geographic Society, 2010.

Potts, Richard, et al. "Environmental Dynamics During the Onset of the Middle Stone Age in Eastern Africa." *Science* 360, no. 6384 (2018): 86–90.

Price, Michael, et al. "Africans, Too, Carry Neanderthal Genetic Legacy." *Science* 367, no. 6477 (2020): 497.

Prüfer, Kay, et al. "A Genome Sequence from a Modern Human Skull over 45,000 Years Old from Zlatý Kůň in Czechia." *Nature Ecology and Evolution* (2021): doi:10.1038/s41559-021-01443-x

Pu, L., et al. "Preliminary Study on the Age of Yuanmou Man by Palaeomagnetic Technique." *Scientia Sinica* 20, no. 5 (1977): 645–664.

Quammen, David. *The Song of the Dodo: Island Biogeography in an Age of Extinction.* New York: Scribner, 1996.

Quammen, David. *The Tangled Tree: A Radical New History of Life.* New York: Simon and Schuster, 2018.

Radovčić, Davorka, et al. "Evidence for Neandertal Jewelry: Modified White-Tailed Eagle Claws at Krapina." *PLOS ONE* 10, no. 3 (2015): e0119802. doi:10.1371.0119802

Raia, Pasquale, et al. "Past Extinctions of *Homo* Species Coincided with Increased Vulnerability to Climate Change." *One Earth* 3, no. 4 (2020): 480–490.

Raichlen, D. A., et al. "Laetoli Footprints Preserve the Earliest Direct Evidence of Human-Like Bipedal Biomechanics." *PLOS ONE* 5, no. 3 (2010): e9769. doi:10.1371/journal.pone.0009769

Reed, D. L., et al. "Pair of Lice Lost or Parasites Regained: The Evolutionary History of Anthropoid Primate Lice." *BioMed Central Biology* 5, no. 7 (2007).[1]

Reich, David. *Who We Are and How We Got Here: Ancient DNA and the New Science of the Human Past.* New York: Vintage Books, 2018.

Reumer, Jelle W. F., et al. "Late Pleistocene Survival of the Saber-Toothed Cat *Homotherium* in Northwestern Europe." *Journal of Vertebrate Paleontology* 23, no. 1 (2003): 260–262.

Rizal, Yan, et al. "Last Appearance of *Homo erectus* at Ngandong, Java, 117,000 to 108,000 Years Ago." *Nature* 577 (2020): 381–385.

Rodgers, Alan R., et al. "Neanderthal-Denisovan Ancestors Interbred with a Distantly Related Hominin." *Science Advances* 6, no. 8 (2020). doi:10.1126/sciadv.aay5483

Ruff, Christopher B., et al. "Body Mass and Encephalization in Pleistocene Homo." *Nature* 387 (1997): 173–176.

---

1   I confess that this reference relates to nothing in the text, since I decided to spare you the results of my dive into the evolution of human head, pubic, and body lice. But it's the best scientific article title *ever*.

Sala, Nohemi, et al. "Lethal Interpersonal Violence in the Middle Pleistocene." *PLOS ONE* 10, no. 5 (2015). doi:10.1371/journal.pone.0126589

Sanz, Crickette, et al. *Tool Use in Animals: Cognition and Ecology.* Cambridge, UK: Cambridge University Press, 2013.

Schaller, George S. *Golden Shadows, Flying Hooves.* New York: Alfred A. Knopf, 1973.

Schaller, George S. *The Serengeti Lion: A Study of Predator-Prey Relations.* Chicago: The University of Chicago Press, 1972.

Schoch, Werner H., et al. "New Insights on the Wooden Weapons from the Paleolithic Site of Schöningen." *Human Evolution* 89 (2015): 214–225.

Schultz, Susanne, et al. "Hominin Cognitive Evolution: Identifying Patterns and Processes in the Fossil and Archeological Record." *Philosophical Transactions of the Royal Society B* 367 (2012): 2130–2140.

Sejnowski, Terrance. "Wired for Intelligence." In *Sydney Brenner's 10-on-10: The Chronicles of Evolution,* edited by Sydney Brenner, 139–149. Singapore: Wildtype Books, 2019.

Senut, B., et al. "First Hominid from the Miocene (Lukeino Formation, Kenya)." *Comptes Rendus de l'Académie des Sciences—Series IIA—Earth and Planetary Science* 332 (2001): 137–144.

Slon, Viviane. "The Genome of the Offspring of a Neanderthal Mother and a Denisovan Father." *Nature* 561 (2018): 113–116.

Smith, Tanya M. *The Tales Teeth Tell: Development, Evolution, Behavior.* Cambridge, MA: The MIT Press, 2018.

Spawls, Stephen, et al. *Field Guide to East African Reptiles.* London: Bloomsbury Natural History, 2018.

Spawls, Stephen, et al. *Reptiles and Amphibians of East Africa.* Princeton, NJ: Princeton University Press, 2006.

Stanford, Craig. *Apes of the Impenetrable Forest: The Behavioral Ecology of Sympatric Chimpanzees and Gorillas.* Upper Saddle River, NJ: Pearson Prentice Hall, 2008.

Stanford, Craig. *The New Chimpanzee: A Twenty-First-Century Portrait of Our Closest Kin.* Cambridge, MA: Harvard University Press, 2018.

Sterelny, Kim. *The Evolved Apprentice: How Evolution Made Humans Unique.* Cambridge, MA: The MIT Press, 2012.

Sterelny, Kim. "Language, Gesture, Skill: The Co-Evolutionary Foundations of Language." *Philosophical Transactions of the Royal Society B* 367 (2012): 2141–2151.

Stewart, Mathew, et al. "Human Footprints Provide Snapshot of Last Interglacial Ecology in the Arabian Interior." *Science Advances* 6, no. 38 (2020). doi:10.1126/sciadv.aba8940

Stout, Dietrich. "Tales of a Stone Age Neuroscientist." *Scientific American,* April 2016, 29–35.

Stout, Dietrich, and Nada Khreisheh. "Skill Learning and Human Brain Evolution: An Experimental Approach." *Cambridge Archeological Journal* 25, no. 4 (2015): 867–875.

Stringer, Chris. "The Origin and Evolution of *Homo sapiens.*" *Philosophical Transactions of the Royal Society B* 371, no. 1698 (2016). doi:10.1098/rstb.2015.0237

Suddendorf, Thomas. *The Gap: The Science of What Separates Us from Other Animals.* New York: Basic Books, 2013.

Sugden, Andrew M., et al. "Dating the Drimolen Hominins." *Science* 368, no. 6486 (2020): 42–44.

Sutikna, Thomas, et al. "The Spatio-Temporal Distribution of Archaeological and Faunal Finds at Liang Bua (Flores, Indonesia) in Light of the Revised Chronology for *Homo floresiensis.*" *Journal of Human Evolution* 124 (2018): 52–74.

Tomasello, Michael. *A Natural History of Human Thinking.* Cambridge, MA: Harvard University Press, 2014.

Trinkaus, Erik, et al. "External Auditory Exostoses Among Western Eurasian Late Middle and Late Pleistocene Humans." *PLOS ONE* (2019). doi:10.1371/journal.pone.0220464

Turner, Alan. *The Big Cats and Their Fossil Relatives*. New York: Columbia University Press, 1997.

Tyler, D. E., and S. Sartono. "A New *Homo erectus* Cranium from Sangiran, Java." *Human Evolution* 16, no. 1 (2001): 13–25.

Unger, Peter S. *Evolution's Bite*. Princeton, NJ: Princeton University Press, 2017.

United Nations Educational, Scientific, and Cultural Organization (UNESCO). "Cueva de las Manos, Río Pinturas." https://whc.unesco.org/en/list/936/

Vanhaeren, Marian, et al. "Middle Paleolithic Shell Beads in Israel and Algeria." *Science* 312, no. 5781 (2006): 1785–1788.

Vignaud, Patrick, et al. "Geology and Palaeontology of the Upper Miocene Toros-Menalla Hominid Locality, Chad." *Nature* 418 (2002): 152–155.

Villa, Paola, et al. "Neandertals on the Beach: Use of Marine Resources at Grotta dei Moscerini (Latium, Italy)." *PLOS ONE* 15, no. 1 (2020). doi:10.1371/journal.pone.0226690

Ward, Carol V., et al. "A Late Miocene Hominid Partial Pelvis from Hungary." *Journal of Human Evolution* 136 (2019). doi:10.1016/j.jhevol.2019.102645

Welker, Fredo, et al. "Enamel Proteome Shows that *Gigantopithecus blacki* Was an Early Diverging Pongine." *Nature* 576 (2019): 262–265.

Wengrow, David. *What Makes Civilization? The Ancient Near East and the Future of the West*. Oxford, UK: Oxford University Press, 2010.

Weyrich, Laura S., et al. "Neanderthal Behavior, Diet, and Disease Inferred from Ancient DNA in Dental Calculus." *Nature* 544 (2017): 357–361.

White, Randall, et al. "Still No Archeological Evidence that Neanderthals Created Iberian Cave Art." *Journal of Human Evolution* 144 (2020). doi:10.1016/j.jhevol.2019.102640

White, Tim, et al. "*Ardipithecus ramidus* and the Paleobiology of Early Hominids." *Science* 326, no. 5949 (2009): 64–86.

Wilifried, Ebang, and Juichi Yamagiwa. "Use of Tool Sets by Chimpanzees for Multiple Purposes in Moukalaba-Doudou National Park, Gabon." *Primates* 55, no. 4 (2014): 467–472.

Wilson, E. O. *The Origins of Creativity*. New York: W. W. Norton and Company, 2017.

World Wildlife Fund. *Living Planet Report 2020: Bending the Curve of Biodiversity Loss*. Gland, Switzerland: World Wildlife Fund, 2020.

Wrangham, Richard. *Catching Fire: How Cooking Made Us Human*. New York: Basic Books, 2009.

Wrangham, Richard. "Control of Fire in the Paleolithic: Evaluating the Cooking Hypothesis." *Current Anthropology* 58, no. S16 (2017): S303–S313. doi:10.1086/692113

Wu, Liu, et al. "The Earliest Unequivocally Modern Humans in Southern China." *Nature* 526 (2015): 696–699.

Wynn, Thomas, et al. "An Ape's View of the Oldowan Revisited." *Evolutionary Anthropology: Issues, News and Reviews* 20, no. 5 (2011): 181–197.

Wynn, Thomas, and John Gowlett. "The Handaxe Reconsidered." *Evolutionary Anthropology: Issues, News and Reviews* 27 (2017): 21–29.

Zhao, L. X., and L. Z. Zhang. "New Fossil Evidence and Diet Analysis of *Gigantopithecus blacki* and Its Distribution and Extinction in South China." *Quarternary International* 286 (2013): 69–74.

Zhu, Zhaoyu, et al. "Hominin Occupation of the Chinese Loess Plateau Since About 2.1 Million Years Ago." *Nature* 559 (2018): 608–612.

Zilhao, J., et al. "Last Interglacial Iberian Neandertals as Fisher-Hunter-Gatherers." *Science* 367, no. 6485 (2020): 1443. doi:10.1126/science.aaz7943

Zink, Katherine D., and Daniel F. Lieberman. "Impact of Meat and Lower Palaeolithic Food Processing Techniques on Chewing in Humans." *Nature* 531 (2016): 500–503.

IMAGE CREDITS

Back cover: buteo/stock.adobe.com.

Front matter: pp. ii–iii: Javier Trueba/MSF/Science Source; pp. vi: Dr. Habiba Chirchir.

Introduction: p. ix: NASA and marcel/stock.adobe.com.

How We Started: p. 3: Martin Harvey/Science Source.

Step 1: p. 8: Kenneth Garrett; p. 16: Javier Trueba/MSF/Science Photo Library; p. 18: Brett Eloff.

Step 2: p. 22: Andy Comins; p. 25: Javier Trueba/MSF/Science Photo Library; p. 29: Sinclair Stammers/ Science Photo Library; p. 32: Human Origins Program, NMNH, Smithsonian Institution.

Step 3: p. 38: Pamela S. Turner; p. 40: Human Origins Program, NMNH, Smithsonian Institution; p. 45: Tony Berlant Collection, Courtesy Nasher Sculpture Center, Dallas; p. 46: John Reader/Science Photo Library.

Step 4: p. 55: Wim Lustenhouwer, VU University Amsterdam, Naturalis Biodiversity Center; p. 56: Pamela S. Turner; p. 60: Kenneth Garrett.

Step 5: p. 65: Denis-Huot/Nature Picture Library/Science Photo Library; p. 71: Philippe Psaila/Science Source; p. 74: Tony Berlant Collection, Courtesy Nasher Sculpture Center, Dallas.

Step 6: p. 79: Ivan Kuzmin/Science Source; p. 80: Department of Archaeology, McGregor Museum, South Africa; p. 87: Javier Trueba/MSF/Science Source; p. 89: Volker Minkus, Niedersächsisches Landesamt fur Denkmalpfiege; p. 90: Reproduced by permission of University of Cambridge Museum of Archaeology and Anthropology (1916.82/Record 2).

Step 7: p. 95: Mohammed Kamal, MPI-EVA Leipzig, License: CC-BY-SA 2.0; p. 98: Human Origins Program, NMNH, Smithsonian Institution; p. 99: C. D. Standish, A. W. G. Pike and D. L. Hoffmann; p. 101: Kenneth Garrett; p. 103: MPI-EVA Leipzig; p. 105: Beawiharta Beawiharta/Reuters/ Alamy Stock Photo; p. 112 (top left): Maxime Aubert, (top right): "Lion Man" sculpture, photo by O. Kuchar, copyright Museum Ulm, (bottom): Javier Trueba/MSF/Science Photo Library; p. 113: Bridgeman Images.

Conclusion: p. 120: Adam Brumm, Ratno Sardi, and Adhi Agus Oktaviana; p. 121 (top): Marcos Diez, (bottom): Wayne Lawler/Science Photo Library; p. 122 (top): David Coulson/Trust for African Rock Art, (bottom): alphacero/stock.adobe.com.

Back matter: p. 131: Javier Trueba/MSF/Science Source.

All map backgrounds: dziewul/stock.adobe.com.

All other art created by John Gurche.

INDEX

Page numbers in italics refer to images or maps.